19.97

The EXPLORER'S GUIDE *to* ALGONQUIN PARK

For Harrison and Dylan.
May wild Algonquin eternally remain for you to explore.

The EXPLORER'S GUIDE to ALGONQUIN PARK

MICHAEL RUNTZ

A Boston Mills Press Book

Copyright © 2008 Michael Runtz
Photographs copyright © 2008 Michael Runtz

First Printing

Library and Archives Canada Cataloguing in Publication
Runtz, Michael W. P.
The explorer's guide to Algonquin Park / Michael Runtz. — Rev. expanded ed.
Includes bibliographical references and index.
ISBN-13: 978-1-55046-498-6
ISBN-10: 1-55046-498-1
1. Algonquin Provincial Park (Ont.) —Guidebooks. I. Title.
FC3065.A65R86 2008   917.13'147   C2007-906820-0

Publisher Cataloging-in-Publication Data (U.S.)
Runtz, Michael W. P.
The explorer's guide to Algonquin Park / Michael Runtz. — Rev. expanded ed.
[224] p. : col. photos., maps ; cm.
Includes bibliographical references and index.
Summary: Access routes to the Algonquin Park including hiking trails and canoe routes,
with narrative on points of historical interest and wildlife.
ISBN-13: 978-1-55046-498-6 (pbk.)
ISBN-10: 1-55046-498-1 (pbk.)
1. Algonquin Provincial Park (Ont.) — Guidebooks.
2. Hiking — Algonquin Provincial Park (Ont.) — Guidebooks.
3. Trails — Algonquin Provincial Park (Ont.) — Guidebooks.
4. Canoes and canoeing — Algonquin Provincial Park (Ont.) — Guidebooks.
I. Title.
917.13147 dc22   F1059.A4.R868 2008

Published by Boston Mills Press, 2008
132 Main Street, Erin, Ontario N0B 1T0
Tel: 519-833-2407 Fax: 519-833-2195

In Canada:
Distributed by Firefly Books Ltd.
66 Leek Crescent, Richmond Hill, Ontario,
Canada L4B 1H1

In the United States:
Distributed by Firefly Books (U.S.) Inc.
P.O. Box 1338, Ellicott Station, Buffalo,
New York 14205

The publisher gratefully acknowledges the financial support of our publishing program the Government of Canada through the Book Publishing Industry Development Program (BPIDP).

Design by Linda Norton-McLaren
Editorial work by Jane McWhinney

Printed in China

The chicks of the common loon leave
the nest immediately after hatching.

CONTENTS

ACKNOWLEDGEMENTS

If I were to list all of the people who have contributed to my knowledge, understanding and appreciation of Algonquin Park, I would need an entire book for that purpose alone. In this limited space I can thank only a portion of those whose names deserve to be here

Above all, I must thank my parents, who first exposed me to Algonquin so many years ago. And then I must thank my sister Karen for driving me to the Park when I was first hired as a licence-less seasonal naturalist. Of course I must thank those who hired me – Dan Strickland and Ron Tozer – who were perhaps misled by an overly enthusiastic Ron Pittaway! These two men, every bit a part of Algonquin as gray jays and wolves, continue to enrich me with their tutelage and friendship. No one knows more or feels more passionately about Algonquin Park than they do, and I consider it a great privilege to know them. I would also like to thank Ron Tozer for reviewing text and offering valuable suggestions for earlier versions of this book.

During my years as an Algonquin Park interpretive naturalist, I had the honour of working alongside many talented people who willingly shared their knowledge of the Park and its natural history with me (as well as other useful knowledge concerning the art of ping pong and darts). Bill Crins and Rory MacKay, in particular, continue to enrich my life with their knowledge, enthusiasm and friendship. Rory also offered many valuable suggestions

for this revision. I would also like to thank Ron Pittaway, Dan Brunton, Paul Pratt, Paul Keddy, Howard Coneybeare, John LeVay, Peter Burke, Colin Jones, Richard Russell, George Fritz, Lisa Enright, Matt Holder and Brad Steinberg for their friendship, sharing of knowledge and special memories. Others to whom I am indebted include current Algonquin Park superintendent, John Winters, former Algonquin Park superintendent Ernie Martelle, former Bonnechere Provincial Park superintendent Jim Fraser, Algonquin Park Chief Park Naturalist, Rick Stronks, Henry and Nancy Checko, Maureen Luckasavitch, Larry Weller, Larry Cobb, Gerhard Shienke, Jack Mihell, Graham Forbes, Kevin Hockley, Dwayne Harty, Peter Smith, Richard Swift and Alison Colotelo. A thank you also to Jane McWhinney and Linda Norton for their skillful contributions to this book, and for their patience with this somewhat forgetful author.

A heartfelt thank you goes to my sons, Harrison and Dylan, who deserve medals for their tolerance of a father who so frequently vanished into the wilds of Algonquin long before they arose, or dragged them out of bed to join him on many an impromptu excursion into the Park.

And last but certainly not least, my heartfelt thanks and love to my fiancée, Ann, for her inspiration, for her help with revisions into the wee hours of the morning (on more than one occasion), and for opening my eyes to yet another, more beautiful side of Algonquin.

Ancient rock and pristine waters dominate the Algonquin landscape.

Many decades have passed since my first visit to Algonquin, when I was brought as a child by my parents to see the autumnal splendour and to feed salted crackers to the white-tailed deer begging for handouts along Highway 60. From that early contact with what is fondly referred to as "the Park" arose an irrepressible obsession that keeps me returning to Algonquin, occasionally in the guise of a working man. For 14 seasons (my, how time flies!) I have worked as a seasonal naturalist, conducting interpretive walks and evening programs at the Outdoor Theatre, the Park Museum and the Algonquin Visitor Centre. Over the years I have worn other hats in Algonquin, including that of canoe-trip permit seller, hawk surveyor, natural history consultant, author, dragonfly counter, canoe tripper, naturalist, television host, sedge photographer, radio co-host, competitive birder, butterfly counter, journalist, Christmas Bird Count participant, artist and university field course instructor.

I must confess … I cannot get enough of this incomparable park. The time spent feeding my addiction has given me a special familiarity with Algonquin that I hope is revealed in this new edition of *The Explorer's Guide to Algonquin Park*. The first edition was released in 1993 with the goal of answering the questions and enhancing the experiences of Park users. Five printings, a partial revision, and myriad positive comments indicate that this goal has been achieved, at least in part. Since the last printing, a number of new trails, services and regulations have arisen, so an updated book is a necessity once again. In this revision I devote more attention to the Park's most valuable asset – its remarkable and diverse natural history.

The primary purpose of this revised edition remains the same – to maximize your enjoyment of Algonquin Park whether it is your first or your hundredth visit. If this book allows you to leave the Park with an additional fond memory or two – or helps you avoid a less than desirable experience during your stay – then it continues to fulfil its purpose.

Happy exploring!

Sunsets in the Park Interior liberate one's soul.

The author as a young boy, held by his father, feeds deer along Highway 60. (Photo: June Runtz).

THE LAY OF THE LAND

More than a century ago Alexander Kirkwood and James Dickson, a government clerk and a land surveyor respectively, recognized the importance of a certain rugged highland area in southern Ontario as the source of major rivers as well as the essential habitat for many types of wildlife. Thanks to their foresight and their appreciation of these special attributes, "Algonquin National Park" was established in 1893. Currently encompassing 7725 km² (3,000 square miles), Algonquin Provincial Park is the oldest and third-largest of Ontario's provincial parks. While its size and age are impressive, other traits are responsible for the special bond that develops between Algonquin and those who meet her. Rugged landscapes, pristine waters and abundant wildlife, the very features that caught the attention of Kirkwood and Dickson, inspire lifelong memories in the near million people who visit Algonquin annually.

Algonquin supports an unusual blend of boreal and southern habitats.

One of the great allures of Algonquin is its wealth of living things. With 276 species of birds (of which 142 have nested in the Park), more than a hundred species of dragonflies and damselflies, 85 species of butterflies, 52 species of mammals (the official count is 51, but I observed a lynx, not on the list, in the Park in 1978), 31 species of reptiles and amphibians, and more than a thousand species of vascular plants, it is impossible to visit without seeing something of interest. Even more striking than the diversity of the flora and fauna is their composition. "Southerners" such as white-tailed deer, scarlet tanagers, red trillium and yellow birch can be found in close proximity to true "northerners" such as moose, spruce grouse, Labrador tea and black spruce. For a naturalist, Algonquin Park is a dream come true.

Why this great and unusual array of flora and fauna? The answer lies largely in the Park's location. Algonquin is situated at the heart of the Great Lakes–St. Lawrence Forest Region, a vast transition zone in which the temperatures and growing season are adequate to support plants whose main range lies either farther north in the Boreal Forest or farther south in the Carolinian Forest. Algonquin's geological history is also a factor. The Park is situated on the top of a batholith, a massive dome of ancient Precambrian rock that was initially formed deep under the earth's surface. Today this dome, with elevations reaching 585 metres (1,900 feet) above sea level, affects Algonquin's temperatures, creating the cooler conditions favoured by many northern plants. The west side of the Park boasts the greatest heights, which average 200 metres (650 feet) higher than those on the east side of Algonquin.

This young great gray owl in a yellow birch near Opeongo Lake sets the most southerly Canadian nesting record of this species.

The glaciers also had an important effect on the composition of today's flora and fauna. When the mile-high blanket of ice and snow last retreated from the western highlands a mere 10,000 years ago, it left behind a layer of rocks, silt, gravel and sand. This mixture of material, known as glacial till, traps moisture, creating conditions suitable for the growth of hardwood trees such as sugar maple, yellow birch and American beech. On north-facing slopes where the environment is cooler, stately stands of eastern hemlocks thrive and cast their shadows all year long. In the autumn their dark green foliage is a counterpoint to the brilliant orange, yellow and red hues of the maple-dominated hills … a blaze of colour that knows no rival.

The east side of Algonquin supports a very different forest. Great beds of sand, deposited by a formidable glacial river that flowed through much of this part of present-day Algonquin, drain moisture away readily. In addition, this region receives less precipitation than the rest of Algonquin because of a slight rain-shadow effect caused by the western highlands. In combination, these factors create dry conditions that favour the growth of softwoods rather than hardwoods. A patchwork quilt of white and red pines, and in some sites jack pines, interspersed with pale trunks of poplars and birches, blankets most of eastern Algonquin.

But coniferous forests are not confined to the eastern regions. Lakeshores all through the Park are fringed with white spruce, balsam fir, eastern white cedar and eastern hemlock. Next to sheltered shores and on top of former ponds, floating mats of sphagnum moss support the spindly spires of black spruce and the delicate contours of tamarack. In a few places, extensive stands of black spruce cloak long-established peatlands.

These different forests support the rich variety of animal life for which Algonquin is famous, including many species synonymous with the Great North. The Park is one of the finest moose-viewing areas in the world, and it boasts one of the most accessible wolf populations anywhere. Marten, fisher, mink, beaver, river otter, white-tailed deer and black bear are all regularly encountered. This abundance of wildlife is a goldmine for the photographer. And I speak from experience.

The forests you see today, although similar in many respects to those admired by the first visitors to the region, differ in one major way. Two centuries ago the western uplands were dotted with towering white pines. These giants captured the attention of the early lumber industry and by the 1830s axes rang all through Algonquin. Thousands of men spent their winters felling pines, stripping off their bark and outer wood in a process known as "squaring," and hauling the squared timbers to frozen lakes. These hardy men cooked, ate and slept in one-room log buildings known as "camboose cabins." The logging

The glacial sand beds of Radiant Lake are most visible at summer's end.

Brewer Lake offers some of the most spectacular views of Algonquin's famed fall colours.

camps broke up in early spring when warm temperatures freed the lakes and rivers from their frozen shackles. Swollen by the spring thaw, Algonquin waterways became living conveyor belts, transporting timbers in "log drives" all the way to larger rivers such as the mighty Ottawa. There were many perils along the way, and crosses marking the graves of unfortunate victims of the spring drives can still be found.

By the late 1800s the supply of big pines had begun to vanish. As the demand for sawn lumber and other materials grew, smaller trees, no doubt scorned by the first loggers, were eagerly harvested. In the ensuing years new logging camps, more modern in construction than the camboose camps over which they were frequently built, sprang up. Logs still flowed down thundering rivers in the spring but now they also left the newly formed "Algonquin National Park" by rail. By this time, in addition to logs, the Ottawa, Arnprior & Parry Sound (OA&PS) Railway, built between 1894 and 1896 by powerful lumber magnate J.R. Booth, transported sawn lumber from mills in the Park. Today, logging still takes place in Algonquin, but the mills are all gone and most of the activity is removed from the public eye.

The early railway carried more than timbers. It brought fishermen and other outdoor enthusiasts, who soon discovered the untapped wealth of the Park's natural resources. As the fame of wild Algonquin spread, lodges were built along the rail line and summer residences sprang up on many of the lakes. Highway 60, built in the mid-1930s, provided alternative access for outdoor recreationists and, eventually, an alternative means of transport for the lumber industry. The importance of the railway quickly faded, however, and in 1946 service from the east was stopped. The great lodges, once thriving enterprises, fell silent and were ultimately dismantled. By 1959 all service along this line, once one of the busiest in Canada, was discontinued and a glorious era came to an end. Now, scattered and often obscure clues are all that remain of those early days.

In 1915 a second railway reached Algonquin. The Canadian Northern Railway, which later became the Canadian National, crossed the northern reaches of the Park, and its trains regularly dropped off canoeists, including the famous artist Tom Thomson (who drowned in Algonquin in 1917) and former Canadian prime minister Pierre  Elliot Trudeau, at popular launching points for trips. Today, the heavy rumble of train wheels no longer echoes off rocky Algonquin shores. The last train on this line passed through in 1995, and over the next few years the steel rails were all removed.

Although Algonquin continues to provide timber to the lumber industry, it has become far more important for outdoor recreation, and presently offers outstanding camping, canoeing,

White pines more than 200 years old still tower overhead in Algonquin, here along the Big Pines Trail.

Algonquin's rich diversity of trees, including these tamaracks in autumn, continues to capture the attention of Park visitors today.

fishing and wildlife-viewing opportunities.
Drive-in campgrounds are found not only along
Highway 60, the main and only access road
crossing the Park, but also at other access points
such as Achray on Grand Lake. With more than
2,100 interior campsites situated along 2000
km (1,250 miles) of established canoe routes
and 140 km (87 miles) of backpacking trails, a
wilder, more private style of camping lures the
adventurous. Fish, most notably speckled and
lake trout, thrive in the clear, cold waters, and
fishermen frequently depart with proof to
support their fantastic stories.

For the explorer who simply appreciates the
beauty of a natural landscape, Algonquin never
disappoints. Throughout the Park, crystal lakes
and winding rivers are fringed with cool, dark
conifers and rugged Precambrian cliffs. After
a cool late-summer night, the lakes at dawn
are alive with mist-shrouded apparitions that
dance across the water until they are banished
by the sun. In autumn, the western hills flame
with colour. As this display begins to fade, the
gold of poplars and tamaracks reigns supreme.
Breathtaking beauty continues in the winter as
sparkling snows create silent splendour under
skies so blue they seem heavy. Throughout
the year the Park presents new personae of
incomparable brilliance and variety.

Algonquin Provincial Park is a very special
place. Although its resources have been exploited
since its inception, the fabric of Algonquin has
survived intact. Loons still serenade the setting
sun, and pines continue to whisper their secrets
to the wind. Today's explorer can marvel at the
natural wonders of the present as well as artifacts
from the past. Welcome to Algonquin. May your
trip be a memorable one.

Interior campsites, such as this
one on Lake Opeongo, are ideal
for viewing Algonquin sunsets.

HARDWOOD FORESTS

The West Side of Algonquin Park, the side that the great majority of visitors are acquainted with, is primarily a sea of sugar maples with yellow birch, red maple, ironwood, American beech, red maple, and black cherry scattered through it. In summer, the hardwood leaves bear little resemblance to those that so vividly paint the western hills in the fall. But it might be surprising to learn that much of the spectacular colour is actually already present in the leaves through the summer, hidden under the cloak of green chlorophyll. Only when the green mask breaks down in September is the colour liberated to our eye. However, some of the intense red that flames in the leaves of male red maple trees (the leaves of the female trees turn yellow) is manufactured as part of the effort to reclaim nutrients that will be lost when the leaves drop lifelessly to the forest floor.

Sugar maples, yellow birch, and other hardwoods on Algonquin's western hills come alive in autumn.

Algonquin hardwood forests are filled with living things, and these exist in stratified layers. In the canopy of leaves high overhead are birds that give you a strained neck when you try to see them. Although the "robin with a sore throat" song of the scarlet tanager, a stunning red-bodied and black-winged bird, is commonly heard, the thick canopy of leaves usually hides its singer. Another invisible voice from above is that of the eastern wood-pewee, a flycatcher that lazily whistles its name.

Black-throated blue warblers, least flycatchers, and melodious veeries and wood thrushes are easier to see, for these birds inhabit the shrub layer, which grows to about eye-level. Beaked hazel is the dominant shrub, and its large fruits attract eastern chipmunks and black bears, which noisily crack them open in late summer. Striped maple, named for its lively green-and-white striped bark, and hobblebush, whose massive paired leaves have earned it the moniker "nature's toilet paper," also thrive as shrubs in the shade of

the hardwood forest. Their huge leaves act like solar panels, capturing and converting into energy the limited light that falls in this habitat.

There is life in the canopy and in the shrubs, and there is life down by your feet. When you visit a hardwood forest in summer and survey the ground cover, you might easily conclude that only young sugar maples live at that level, for there is a sea of them. Unless a hole in the canopy permits more light to reach the forest floor, this army of maple seedlings dies after several years. Weep not for the loss, however, for other seedlings immediately take their place. Thus, whenever an aged maple succumbs to the years and tumbles to the ground, new recruits to reclaim the gap in the canopy are always ready and willing.

Although in summer it might seem that nothing but green maple leaves grows at ground level, from late April through mid-May, splashes of trout-lily yellow, red-trillium burgundy, Dutchman's-breeches white, and spring-beauty pink greet the eye. A virtual bouquet of spring

The scarlet tanagers that nest in Algonquin spend their winters in Brazil.

Like other shrubs and trees, beaked hazel unpredictably produces large crops of fruit only in certain years.

flowers blooms early to exploit the uninhibited sunlight. After the show of blooms is over, the flowers' leaves hide the domed nests of ovenbirds. While you may never see the nest of an ovenbird, you will likely hear its "teacher, teacher, teacher" song ringing loudly through the forest.

Once the tree leaves have opened overhead, the habitat becomes a shady retreat in which very few flowers bloom. Wood sorrel is a noteworthy exception. Another is Indian pipe, whose ghostly white stalks arise mysteriously in late summer. This flower, with its resemblance to a fungus, has lost all need for sunlight. Its roots have fungal associates that bring it sustenance stolen from the roots of nearby trees.

Every part of the hardwood forest provides habitat or food for other living things. The leaves of maples are devoured by hosts of caterpillars, and in late summer they often bear the odd vertical spikes of spindle gall mites or the plush red carpets of pile mites. The seeds of the maples and other hardwoods are important food for

eastern chipmunks, deer mice and woodland jumping mice. The latter are strictly nocturnal and are one of the three true hibernators found in Algonquin (meadow jumping mice and groundhogs are the others). Other creatures, such as black bears and eastern chipmunks, fail to experience the complete drop in body temperature and heart rate that true hibernators experience during their much longer periods of inactivity.

The unusual triangular nuts of the American beech are housed in spiny husks that pose no problem for black bears, and in late summer, as they fatten up for winter dormancy, these shy creatures climb beech trees to feast on them. The largest beech trees are inevitably marked with distinctive blackened claw scars left as permanent mementos by foraging bears, as well as with unsightly tangles of broken limbs known as "bear nests."

Older trees draw the attention of wood-eating beetles, which in turn catch the eyes and highly extensible tongues of woodpeckers. The giant of its group, the crow-sized pileated woodpecker, roams the hardwoods in search of carpenter ants, leaving rectangular excavations as testaments to particularly good feeding sites. Old trees become riddled with cavities and are nothing short of high-rise apartments as they provide

nesting and den sites for northern flying squirrels, raccoons, fishers, white-breasted nuthatches, great crested flycatchers and barred owls. Ducks also vie for vacancies: wood ducks, and common and hooded mergansers are all cavity nesters.

Once age topples a tree, the fallen trunk becomes a "nursery log" for the seeds of yellow birch and eastern hemlock. When the logs become soft and soggy with age, female red-backed salamanders hang their baskets of eggs inside them, staying to guard their offspring until they hatch. Time and fungus eventually work their magic, leaving only elongated mounds or yellow birches perched tippy-toed on their exposed roots as epitaphs to an old log.

In earlier days the giant white pines that towered above the maples were a component of Algonquin's hardwood forests. These trees, which the first loggers felled by hand and sent to England to be used as masts for sailing ships, are almost all gone from the forests of today. However, a few examples of old-growth pines still stand in remote locations such as Dividing Lake and the Crow River. Fortunately for the park visitor who has neither the time nor the inclination to paddle and portage a canoe for several days, a number of these magnificent old trees still cast their long shadows over the Big Pines Trail on Highway 60.

Hardwood forests teem with life in spring and summer but in winter the absence of leaves usually results in a scarcity of birds and mammals. If you want to encounter animals during an Algonquin winter, you will have much better luck if you snowshoe through a coniferous forest.

A number of the self-guiding trails located along Highway 60 take you through mature tracts of hardwood forest. Perhaps the best to take is the Hardwood Lookout Trail, for not only does it pass through a magnificent forest but its habitat is nicely interpreted in its trail guide booklet. Whiskey Rapids, Mizzy Lake, Track and Tower, and Booth's Rock trails also take you through fine examples of this habitat. When the autumnal splendour of the sugar maples is at its finest, Hardwood Lookout, Booth's Rock, Centennial Ridges and Lookout trails provide scenic vantage points with breathtaking views.

Dutchman's breeches are one of the many spring ephemerals in western hardwood forests.

Pileated woodpeckers are related to the ivory-billed woodpecker, whose existence in North America is currently a point of debate.

PINE FORESTS

Although you can find respectable patches of white and red pines along Highway 60, particularly in the Mew Lake and Opeongo Lake regions, these pale in comparison to the scope of the pine forests located on the east side of Algonquin, where they cover the terrain with a year-round blanket of green. In some areas where sand plains dominate this part of Algonquin, hardy fire-dependent jack pines also form extensive stands.

Unlike hardwood forests, pine forests offer little seasonal relief from the shade cast by tall trees. Persistent shade, high acidity due to fallen pine needles, and dry conditions (the East Side experiences a small rain-shadow effect from the western uplands and is dominated by sand that drains easily) combine to create conditions unfavourable for most of the hardwood forest spring ephemerals such as red trillium and Dutchman's breeches. However, Algonquin pine forests are by no means flowerless. Many floral gems arise from the underlying carpet of pine needles, feather moss and grey reindeer lichen, the latter crunching loudly underfoot when hot, dry weather prevails. Fringed polygala, Canada mayflower, trailing arbutus and pink lady's-slipper, with its enlarged pouch that traps visiting bees and forces them to pollinate the flower during their escape, all add beauty to an Algonquin pine forest.

East Side lakeside hills are blanketed with pines.

Plants that grow under pines tend to have large leaves for capturing the reduced amount of sunlight that reaches the forest floor. A fine example is clintonia, which has a handful of smooth wide leaves. Other plants, such as bunchberry with its explosive trip-wire flowers, and a variety of clubmosses, accomplish the same feat by bearing many leaves and growing in colonies. When you see a group of bunchberries, note how the stems that bear flowers or fruit have six leaves while the non-flowering stems have only four.

The leaves of deciduous trees are food for animals small and large, and pine needles certainly play that role too. While hardwood leaves are eaten by caterpillars, especially those of moths, the needles of coniferous trees, despite being well armed with nasty chemicals (especially terpenoids), are particularly enjoyed by the larvae of a group of wasps known as sawflies. These look very much like butterfly or moth caterpillars but sport more than four pairs of prolegs. Sawfly larvae and other pine-eating insects are meals for pine warblers and blue-headed vireos, whose loud songs drift down from hidden perches. The cones of pines harbour nutritious seeds that fuel the appetites of red squirrels, red-breasted nuthatches and red crossbills, all of which can usually be found year-round in this habitat. The latter use their peculiar name-giving bills to pry open the scales on pinecones. Once the scale is lifted, the crossbill, with the dexterity of a parrot, employs its tongue to pluck out the seeds. Crossbills and other seed-eating finches frequently pick grit (which is used in the gizzard to grind down the tough seeds) from the road, making them vulnerable to being hit by cars, particularly in winter.

Unlike a pine plantation with its undernourished and overcrowded trees lined up like prisoners under inspection, an Algonquin pine forest is a less constricted and more diverse habitat that contains a scattering of other tree species, most notably trembling aspen, large-tooth poplar and red maple. These sponsor a host of animals, such as the spectacular luna moth, whose caterpillar dines on poplar leaves, and ruffed grouse, which prefer fresh poplar buds.

The Basin Road and the short side road that takes you into Basin Lake pass through lovely pine forests. The Basin Road also brings you through two areas of jack pines: one starts right at the Algonquin boundary sign; the other a couple of kilometres before the hydro line junction near the end of public access. Farther northeast, the Barron Canyon Road winds through many kilometres of this habitat, including an extensive area of jack pine near Lake Travers. Both the Eastern Pines Backpacking Trail and the Berm Lake Trail, whose trail guide booklet interprets the ecology of this habitat, meander through terrific pine forests, as does the top part of the Barron Canyon Trail, which offers a spectacular elevated overview of the pine-ridged canyon.

One trip to the East Side of Algonquin will surely leave you pining to return the following year!

Red crossbills, like other Algonquin finches, eat grit from the roads to aid their digestion of seeds.

In their pouch-like lower petal, pink lady's-slippers have a narrow slit that is the door through which their bee pollinators enter.

Red-headed pine sawflies, not native to North America, thrive where pines are common.

NORTHERN CONIFERS AND PEATLANDS

One of the most visually and biologically interesting aspects of Algonquin is the presence of northern conifers and floating peatlands. The Park's elevated position on top of the roots of an ancient mountain range provides cooler temperatures that favour the growth of northern plants and the formation of northern habitats. It is the colder Algonquin climate that allows spindly black spruce and spire-topped balsam fir to border many lakes and ponds. The cooler temperatures and the acidic nature of Algonquin (due to its backbone of acidic Precambrian granitic and gneissic rock) combine to provide the ideal conditions for the formation of peatlands. Where the water current weakens, floating mats of sedge and moss creep out from the shore, completely smothering the water over time.

Algonquin has its fair share of bogs and fens, the two main types of peatland. The difference between the two lies in the way water and its load of nutrients enter the habitat. If moving surface water, such as a stream, carries nutrients through the peatland, it is technically a fen. If the only input of water (and therefore of nutrients) is through rainfall, then it is a bog. As fens receive more nutrients than bogs do, they tend to be richer habitats, although some fens, especially those in Algonquin, receive low levels of nutrients, so they are known as "poor fens." Over time, a peatland can eventually choke off all flow of water, and thus a fen can become a bog. Also, some parts of the peatland may be affected by flowing water while other parts are not.

Thus, a peatland might be at one time both a bog and a fen, and could change characteristics as time passes. If defining a peatland sounds difficult, it is! Even ecologists don't always agree on naming peatlands, and some argue that the habitat's acidity or dominant plants should be used to determine its classification. Regardless of the titles we give them, peatlands are complex and fascinating habitats to visit.

Wolf Howl Pond on the Mizzy Trail contains a beautiful example of a peatland, this one a donut bog.

Hailstorm Creek is one of the most extensive peatlands in Algonquin.

In Algonquin peatlands, sphagnum mosses are the key players. This seemingly innocuous group of plants actually has the power to colonize open water and transform it into a peatland. The water-holding mosses begin this transformation by attaching to a latticework of floating sedge stems and growing out from the shore. As soon as sphagnum becomes established, it starts working its magic. New moss grows on top of dead moss and this ever-thickening mat cuts off the flow of oxygen and nutrients from the water beneath. The moss absorbs bases and releases humic acids, rendering the new habitat increasingly acidic. Sphagnum moss also acts like a sponge, absorbing water from below and locking it inside its system of hollow dead cells. Eventually, it creates a waterlogged, oxygen-deprived, acidic environment – a most unpleasant habitat by most plants' standards.

Despite the inhospitable conditions, a number of striking plants thrive in Algonquin peatlands. Several of these have evolved a most ingenious means of obtaining nutrients. Pitcher-plants, sundews (there are two types in Algonquin – round-leaved and spatulate-leaved), and no fewer than seven species of bladderworts, which possess submerged lethal bladder traps, capture insects and digest their bodies for the nutrients they contain!

Other plants, such as the colourful sheep and bog laurels, and several stunning orchids including rose pogonia and grass pink, employ fungal pipelines to draw in nutrients from farther afield (or should that be "abog"?). Speckled alder, the dominant shrub that grows on peatland edges and along most Algonquin shorelines, houses nitrogen-fixing bacteria in golden nodules on its roots.

The youngest portion of the floating mat, the part closest to the water, has the greatest richness of plants. Here, the moss is less established, nutrients (carried by the water) are most plentiful and sunlight is not yet blocked by taller plants. The edge is also the most treacherous part of the peatland, for the floating mat is at its most undeveloped stage. I have vivid memories of photographing flowers in this zone and feeling water rise above my knees as the mat slowly sank under my weight … or taking a careless step and suddenly finding moss under my armpits and nothing but water under my feet.

With time, the mat becomes more substantial and sprouts meadows of leatherleaf, whose white bell-like flowers appear in early spring. Hardy conifers start to appear, especially near the former shoreline. Black spruce has no aversion to getting its feet wet, and most peatlands are, at the very least, encircled by these northerners. While the largest black spruce generally stand nearest the former shore, smaller spruce, resembling pawns in front of larger, more powerful pieces, advance toward the younger parts of the mat. Young spruce are often vegetative clones of the older trees behind them, arising from their lower branches that rested on the sphagnum bed.

In the partial shade of the scattered spruces Labrador tea inevitably thrives. The fuzzy orange hairs covering the underside of this plant's leaves help prevent them from drying out, even when winter winds blow across the open peatland. This plant, like many peatland species, retains its leaves year-round, a strategy to preserve the nutrients that are so hard to come by in the peatland habitat.

A black spruce peatland is a delight to roam through. A soft damp carpet of sphagnum cushions your feet and a refreshing coolness escorts you as you make your way through the spindly spruces. Hidden in the trees, Nashville warblers and yellow-bellied flycatchers broadcast their presence. Gray jays, which are easier to see, announce their bold arrival with short hollow whistles. These gentle birds usually need little coaching to accept edible offerings right from your hand. Spruce grouse, also fearless, flutter up into the conifers with a noisy burst of wings. These northern grouse live year-round in this habitat, devouring the needles of the black spruce in all seasons.

In late summer eastern wolves bring their pups to spruce bogs. When the adults return with food and reunite with the pups, haunting howls fill the air. Later, from mid-September to early October, loud moans can be heard from this same habitat, as moose "spruce" up their sexual escapades.

In winter the northern conifers are lifelines for most of the creatures that remain active in Algonquin. The seeds in their cones satiate white-winged crossbills and red squirrels, and their bark harbours beetles that are food for black-backed and American three-toed woodpeckers. Their evergreen needles are favourites of spruce grouse and their snowy branches offer warm roost sites for small birds and sheltered passage for mammals beneath.

Spruce bogs and fens give the rugged Algonquin landscape a deliciously northern flavour. May global warming not rob the Park of these great treasures, for without peatlands and the northern conifers, Algonquin and all those who visit her would be poorer indeed.

Bog copper butterflies live in bogs and fens where rose pogonia orchids also thrive.

Dewdrops, mist and spider webs combine to paint a dramatic sunrise scene at West Rose Lake.

ALGONQUIN LAKES

From trickling streams to more than a thousand sparkling lakes, Algonquin is blessed with myriad waterways. Some of the lakes are so small they pass for ponds; others so huge they look and feel more like small seas from the vantage point of a canoe. When angered by storms, the largest, such as Opeongo, are best left unchallenged; on occasion, some who are foolish enough to try unfortunately fail to complete their journeys.

Algonquin lakes tend to be deep and slightly acidic due to the nature of the rock that defines them. The deep, cold water is ideal for trout, and lake and speckled trout abound. All but the smallest lakes are home to at least one pair of common loons, whose wild calls are an important part of the soul of this wild and beautiful place. Female common mergansers, often confused with loons, also lead their young around the lakes in summer. If the crested head does not allow you to distinguish this common tree-nesting duck from a platform-nesting loon, the dozen or more young in tow should, for loons usually have at most two chicks with them. Another point to

Fork Lake, a mere stone's throw from the Visitor Centre, is testament to Algonquin's wild spirit.

Pickerel-weed flowers are alive with bees, not pickerel!

For common loons, courtship begins as soon as the pair arrives on its territory.

In August, cold nights and warm days are a perfect formula for mist-shrouded sunrises.

separate the two species – loons stay in pairs and share parental duties, but male mergansers, which sport a green head and white body, go north for the summer, saddling the females with all familial responsibilities. While they have their differences, loons and mergansers share two things: a diet of fish and the trait of giving their small young rides on their backs.

The water nearest the shores of lakes can be the most enjoyable part to canoe along, for the shallows support the greatest diversity of life. Here, the leaves and flowers of water-shield, white water-lilies and bullhead-lilies float on the surface, attracting the attention of moose, which spend hours devouring the stems and leaves of these sodium-rich plants.

In the evening, beavers munch away on the same plant material. They also dive to the bottom and break off pieces of root, which they bring to the surface to enjoy.

Nearer to shore in even shallower water, where waves regularly create currents not unlike those found in a stream, stand the odd stick stems of pipewort with their little white floral caps. Also standing erect are bur-reeds with their even stranger seed spike-balls. On occasion the purple flower spikes of pickerelweed are so densely packed that they complain as your canoe passes through them. This beautiful plant bears a most misleading name, for pickerel (alias walleye) are only found in a few of the northeastern lakes in Algonquin. Fishermen are far more apt to find smallmouth bass lurking among the submerged stems of these plants. Unlike pickerel, bass are not native to Algonquin but were introduced in the early days of the railway. The early releases were successful, and today this species thrives in many Algonquin lakes.

The shores themselves are home to a great many plants and animals. Great blue herons slowly stalk the shallows, their long dagger beaks

ready to snare an unwary frog. Mink patrol the shorelines for the same prey. Spotted sandpipers, among the few shorebirds to nest in Algonquin, bob their short tails incessantly as they teeter across the rocks. In addition to their odd walk, these sandpipers have a most unusual nesting behaviour; the females choose several mates, each of which incubates a set of her eggs.

With so many lakes, Algonquin offers a vast range of possibilities for a canoeist (or kayaker). All Algonquin access points take you to at least one lake, and the Highway 60 Corridor offers easy access to no fewer than 21 lakes, many with drive-in campgrounds. One of these, Peck Lake, is encircled by an interpretive walking trail with a trail guide booklet whose theme just happens to be lake ecology.

Lakes are not just inanimate objects that add beauty to Algonquin. They are living entities that change moods frequently. At dawn, misty wraiths slowly waltz across their surface. At day's end their water incandesces orange, gold, red and purple. Under the watchful eye of the moon, their waves lap the shores with a soothing rhythm that carries you into your dreams. On calm summer days they mirror the clouds so perfectly you feel as if you were canoeing in the sky. And then their demeanour can suddenly change. During spring and autumn storms, Algonquin lakes can churn and boil with the fury of an angered Poseidon.

RIVERS AND STREAMS

Algonquin's rivers and streams lack the multiple personalities of her lakes. While the moving waters swell in spring when melting snows and rains add intensity to their flow, little other change is detectable through the seasons. For most of the year their waters flow smoothly and steadily, with an occasional gentle scamper down a set of shallow rapids or an exhilarating tumble down a boulder-strewn waterfall.

Reliable currents are exploited by a number of creatures that extract their food from the oxygen-rich water. If you look at the bottom while passing through shallow rapids, you can easily see them. Attached to rocks are the small, trumpet-shaped webs of net-spinning caddisflies, often numbering in the hundreds. The trumpet opens into the current so that the net can filter out the food for its inhabitant, which lives behind the bend of the trumpet's neck. Not far from these ingenious restaurants are the peculiar near-fluorescent green mounds of freshwater sponges, colonial animals that also receive nutrition by extracting food from the water. Sometimes a colony encrusts a stick, making it look like a colourful finger. If you pick up a sponge-encrusted rock or stick, feel its crusty skeleton and be sure to give it a sniff – its distinctive odour reminds me of the sea.

Look at the underside of a submerged rock and you will find other current dwellers. The flat bodies of stonefly larvae and the silk-and-pebble cases of other caddisfly larvae cling to the submerged rocks. The tiny bodies of young black flies are fascinating when they dangle out into the current, anchored by a silk anchor attached to the rock ... but only then! From their heads, facing downstream, a pair of elegant brushes sweep open and closed, bringing captured organic particles into their mouths.

If you lift up a rock to examine its inhabitants, be sure to return it to its original location. Never pile rocks to build one of those popular Innukshuks in an Algonquin stream, or anywhere for that matter. Removing rocks from their natural position robs many creatures of their essential habitat, which can be very hard to come by. If you find one of these structures already made by someone less informed, do the creatures a favour and return the rocks to the rapids in which they belong.

As you paddle down an Algonquin stream or slow-moving river, you pass by many plants with long, flexible stems that bend and flow with the

Brigham Chute is a beautiful barrier to bypass when one is canoeing downstream to the Barron Canyon.

current. The large clumps of swaying bulrush are mesmerizing. Their dense mats of yellowish-green stems and leaves gently pulsate in the current as if they were a woman's hair being caressed by the water. The leaves of pondweeds also meander across the surface, never travelling far because their roots remain anchored in the bottom. These leaves are narrow and elongate, a shape designed to reduce the drag created by the water flowing around them. Powdered dancers, small damselflies with plenty of whitish bloom on the body, often use them as landing platforms, occasionally crawling off to insert their eggs into the underwater stems. Also watch for the stunning

river jewelwings with emerald bodies and half-black wings, the latter feature distinguishing this species from ebony jewelwings, which have solid black wings.

You are seldom alone when you paddle an Algonquin river. As you round a bend, a great blue heron may flush, and flush again at the next bend, leading you to believe these great birds are as common as the dragonflies that leave you in their aerial wake.

The fastest dragonflies are the clubtails, named for the pronounced swelling of the last few abdominal segments. The largest is the impressive dragonhunter, so named because of its penchant for eating smaller members of its group. My favourite is the zebra clubtail, a dazzling yellow and black speedster that likes a bit of flow in the water it patrols.

The period from late April to mid-May is an excellent time to visit an Algonquin river, for then the water is at its highest and the waterfalls thunder their mightiest. Another not insignificant benefit is that larval black flies have not yet transformed into their bloodletting adult stage. High Falls on the York River, High Falls on the Barron River, and High Falls on the Bonnechere River (do I detect a lack of creativity in naming falls?) can all be accessed by foot. However, if you wish to see impressive Brigham Chute on the Barron River, then a little canoeing and portaging are required. Ragged Falls on the Oxtongue River is also well worth a visit. Although not in Algonquin – it lies a mere 10 km (6 miles) west of the Park – the waters that plunge down this stunning falls come from Algonquin, and it is very easily accessed from Highway 60.

While all of Algonquin's waters are pure and clean, smaller streams may give you a very different impression, for they are often tea-coloured and could lead you to think something has gone terribly wrong. Rest assured that all is fine. The brown colour simply reflects higher levels of organic matter, all due to Algonquin's natural acidity and slower rates of decomposition in the habitats through which many waters flow.

With lethal patience, great blue herons wait for fish or frogs to make an ill-advised move.

While Poplar Rapids on the Petawawa River mumbles in mid-summer, in early spring it roars.

BEAVER PONDS

Of all Algonquin's aquatic habitats, beaver ponds are admittedly my favourite. Unlike small lakes (which beavers also inhabit), a beaver pond is shallow and supports a much larger variety of life. The experience of sitting quietly at a beaver pond at sunrise, the best time for viewing animals, is like watching a fine play. There are a great many characters, each making an appearance of varying length. Some speak no lines: as if painted onto the shore, great blue herons stand silent and motionless, waiting for a frog or a bullhead to make a fatal move; painted turtles sprawl on floating logs, their necks and legs stretched wide to maximize exposure to the sun, which warms them and drives off their parasites.

Other creatures enter with fanfare: a snap of branches followed by loud splashing reveals that a moose has waded into the pond for a meal of water-shield; loud snorts of indignation accompany a troupe of river otters that twist and dive with the grace of seals. And then there is the delightful music of the Beaver Pond Symphony. Green frogs on banjos, black-backed woodpeckers on drums, gray tree frogs on percussion, and veeries and hermit thrushes on wind instruments accompany bullfrogs as they bellow out their baritone melodies. Every now and again, as startling as the unanticipated clash of cymbals, the slap of a beaver's tail punctuates the chorus.

A pond's occupancy by beavers is not always obvious to the eye. Although all beavers build lodges, not always are these houses surrounded by water. Some are placed on the shore and are visible only from certain angles to scrutinizing eyes. Other signs, some quite subtle, can also reveal the presence of these remarkable rodents. Sticks stripped of their bark, either floating in the water or lying on flattened feeding platforms, are a giveaway, as are floating fragments of half-eaten water-lily roots. Fresh mud applied to a lodge or dam, or piled on the shore as a scent post to declare territorial holdings, is also a conclusive sign. Of course, the sighting of a beaver is the best clue to occupancy you could possibly find!

While you may not see beavers on every visit, their ponds are excellent places for encountering animals in general. Ducks are inevitably present; American black ducks, ring-necked ducks (better named "ring-billed ducks"), wood ducks and

Beaver dams create one of the most important habitats in Algonquin.

hooded mergansers, which use their narrow, serrated bills for grabbing small minnows and dragonfly nymphs, all feed and nest in beaver ponds. The latter two species nest in trees drowned by the pond. Dead trees also attract black-backed woodpeckers and northern flickers, which, unlike the ducks, excavate their own homes in the wood. Once vacant, woodpecker homes are quickly usurped by tree swallows, great crested flycatchers, northern saw-whet owls, and even northern flying squirrels.

Beaver ponds harbour more plants than lakes do because their water is shallower, warms more quickly and contains more nutrients. The ponds act as collecting basins for nutrients, some of which arrive with the incoming stream and get deposited when it slows to a crawl upon reaching that infamous obstruction built by the beavers – the dam. A dam does more than slow down the current. It also causes the stalled water to rise and flood the land, which then releases its stored nutrients into the pond. Beavers contribute, too, by dragging plants into the pond and discarding the uneaten portions in the water. They also defecate in the pond, not only making its water richer in nutrients but also rendering it a very unwise source of liquid for quenching your thirst.

Bullhead-lilies, white water-lilies and water-shield thrive in the warm, shallow, and nutrient-rich water of a beaver pond. Their roots, stems, leaves and flowers provide food for moose and beavers. The floating leaves are also eaten by several insects, including waterlily leaf beetles, which decorate them with an incredible maze of patterns as they dine.

Some plants prefer to grow along the damp shore. Jewelweed, with its stunning orange, sex-changing flowers, is also known as "touch-me-not" because of its explosive seedpods. These delightful flowers often grow alongside Joe-Pye weed on old beaver dams, which serve as natural bridges for raccoons, moose, black bears and eastern wolves.

When beavers abandon a pond, the dam eventually breaches and the pond goes dry. A pond and all its inhabitants may vanish but a new habitat will arise in its place. The organically rich mud is soon carpeted with a lush meadow of grass and sedge. This green backdrop is enlivened by the blooms of steeplebush, Joe-Pye weed and swamp milkweed, whose scents and colours attract butterflies galore. In late summer wolf pups romp through the newly formed meadow, and in the early autumn moose use the open space for their age-old rituals of love.

As time passes, shrubs and, ultimately, trees reclaim the land. Then, decades – perhaps centuries – later, beavers may well return to dam the stream and flood the area. When they do, the beaver pond cycle begins anew.

Beavers eat most of their meals in the safety of the water.

Bullhead-lilies adorn shallow waters of ponds and lake edges.

OBSERVING WILDLIFE

Algonquin is famous for the abundance and variety of its wildlife, the result of the mixture of southern and northern habitats. For many visitors, the "must sees" include moose, common loons, beavers, gray jays and eastern wolves, although the latter are primarily a "must hear." Algonquin is quite often the place where a person first meets one or more of these animals.

First-time visitors are sometimes concerned about the danger posed by wild animals and frequently ask: "Are there any dangerous animals in Algonquin Park?" In my opinion, there are none. Although Massasaugas (small rattlesnakes) are found west of Algonquin, they unfortunately do not occur in the Park. I say "unfortunately" because it would be fantastic to have these rare and relatively harmless reptiles as part of its fauna. Algonquin is too cold for these fascinating snakes; the elevations that allow for the formation of boreal bogs are also responsible for the exclusion of many animals.

Eastern wolves use beaver meadows and other open areas as rendezvous sites into late fall.

As a rule, the larger mammals that roam Algonquin are harmless. Some people are concerned about black bears, but these animals are usually quite shy and very difficult to see. It is even more challenging to get a glimpse of an eastern wolf. But on rare occasions a bold individual bear or wolf has been encountered. For more information on these rare encounters, please read the sections that deal specifically with these species. If you are camping, you can virtually eliminate the possibility of having a bear disturb you at night by keeping your campsite free of food after meals, by hanging your food pack out of a bear's reach and by never having food in your tent. The danger you face on the highway in driving to and from Algonquin exceeds by light years any danger posed by black bears or any other of the Park's wild inhabitants.

Although you can encounter many of Algonquin's animals by driving the roads or walking the trails, there are a few "tricks" that will substantially increase your chances of encountering them during your visit to the park. Since each species is usually found in a specific habitat at a certain time of the year, a knowledge of the animal's life history will certainly aid you in your efforts. I highly recommend that you obtain the Algonquin Park publications on wildlife before your visit. These are inexpensive and provide an excellent overview of the animals. (See page 215, "Relevant Publications.")

In earlier years when the moose population was growing, most cows produced twins every spring.

Wildlife-viewing Etiquette

Before I begin suggestions for finding some of the Park's wildlife, I feel that a short treatise on wildlife-viewing etiquette is essential. Far too often, in the excitement of seeing a wild animal up close for the first time or obtaining the ultimate photograph, the viewer's effect on the animal is overlooked. Algonquin's animals, no matter how tame they might seem, are indeed *wild* animals. A lack of consideration for an animal can cause it unnecessary stress and can also put you in danger. Despite the oblivious look on the moose contentedly slurping salty water from the roadside ditch, that 450 kg (1,000-pound) giant can easily crush your skull with one kick of its great hoof. The most important rule to follow is: *Give all animals respect.* If a moose seems absurdly tame, why risk your life by testing its approachability to the limit? Now, I'm not trying to create the impression that these animals are dangerous and that one should be wary of them. Normally they are non-aggressive. But can we predict a moose's behaviour when a crowd of 50 curious observers begins to swarm around it? The animal could panic and run through the group. If young calves are present, the mother might perceive a threat to her offspring and react instinctively and defensively. Bulls can be downright ornery during the fall mating season. So play it safe by playing it smart. Here are a few simple rules to follow:

- Never approach any wild animal too closely. Although it is impossible to prescribe the appropriate viewing distance, a general rule is to stay back at least 20 metres (60 feet) from the larger animals.

- Never lure or chase an animal onto a road where it might be hit by a vehicle (thereby endangering not only the animal but also the occupants of the vehicle).

- Never harass wildlife by repeatedly playing recordings of their sounds or by imitating them in an effort to attract them or keep them close by. If you are trying to get a barred owl, spruce grouse, moose, or eastern wolf to respond to a recording or an imitation, only use the play back or call a few times. Once successful, enjoy the response without attempting to elicit an encore.

- Avoid shining powerful search beams into the eyes of animals at night. Some of these lights generate a tremendous glare that can potentially damage the light-sensitive eyes of nocturnal animals.

- Although feeding gray jays and eastern chipmunks is acceptable, larger animals, particularly black bears and eastern wolves, must never be fed.

- Do not disturb nesting birds, including loons. If a bird is repeatedly flushed off its nest, odds are that the nesting attempt will fail.

- If you encounter an unusually tame black bear or eastern wolf, frighten it off by making loud noises, and if necessary, by throwing objects at it. Never turn your back and run, and never play dead if approached by a bear. Immediately report the encounter to a Park official. Please be aware, however, that this sort of encounter is exceptionally rare.

The antlers of the bull moose are for more than display; they also help bulls tune in to the love calls of distant cows.

When and How to See Wildlife

For viewing most wildlife, the time of day is very important. Dusk arouses nocturnal animals. Dawn instigates a flurry of feeding activity in diurnal animals. Thus, the best time to look for animals is generally either the two or three hours following sunrise, or the hour or two preceding sunset. I prefer the hours that immediately follow the predawn glow. Not only is this one of the best times for wildlife activity but it is also one of the most beautiful times of day. On cool mornings

the glow of the sun warms your cheeks and seems to penetrate your soul. In late summer, spectacular mists shroud the waterways and other low-lying places. In the early morning you feel a special closeness to the Park, a sensation that is difficult to put into words. And when you return to your breakfast table, the coffee and eggs taste extra good!

Since the behaviour of animals changes from season to season, learning a bit about their habits before your visit will increase your chances of encountering them. Contrary to popular thinking, for example, the best way to locate beavers is not to watch for them cutting down trees. During the summer in Algonquin, water plants form an important part of their diet. Thus, beavers are most easily found by scanning the floating leaves of water-lilies and other pond plants for a blunt-shaped head sticking up among them. As these rodents become their most active

toward sunset, watch also for the distinctive V-shaped wake of one plying the surface of a lake.

Your behaviour in the woods is also a factor. Move quietly and slowly. Avoid brightly coloured clothing. If you sit silently for prolonged periods at the edges of habitats at the peak times for animal activity, you will be amazed at how much more you will see. To those who are patient, nature reveals itself wonderfully.

An area that encompasses the borders of several different habitats often produces the greatest variety of animals. Excursions to the edges of beaver ponds, lakes and larger bogs at the optimal times of day, for example, usually reap the greatest rewards. You can also enhance your viewing opportunities with a few simple tricks. If you are looking for birds, an easily made series of sounds is virtually guaranteed to draw them closer for better viewing. Try making the sound *shhhhh*, and add a "p" at the beginning. The resulting noise is known as "pishing" or "spishing." By repeating *pshhhhh* in a short sequence (i.e., *pshhhhh, pshhhhh, pshhhhh, pshhhhh*), you should achieve amazing results. This call resembles the alarm calls of small birds and can elicit a "mobbing" response in the birds that hear it. (Birds often mob sedentary predators such as owls, perhaps to make it safer at night when they are roosting and the owls are hunting.) Try "pishing" in quiet spots along trails or near forest edges. One word of warning, however. People who encounter you making that noise are inevitably curious and yell, "What are you doing?" Never shout back, "Just pishing." You just might be misunderstood!

Another call that attracts larger birds, particularly hunters such as owls and hawks, also serves to attract red foxes, weasels (including martens and fishers), and occasionally even eastern wolves. The sound is a squeal produced by

noisily sucking on the knuckles of your index and middle fingers of one hand. It works best with wet knuckles, so when I lick them first, I achieve a better squeal. The resulting noise, known as "squeaking," is similar to the sound made by an injured prey and, like steel to a magnet, hunters are attracted to what they think is an easy meal. Don't expect results every single time you squeak, however. For this call to work, the predator must be within earshot and must not have been alarmed by your presence.

Imitations of the sounds of a specific animal will frequently entice that species to respond. Perhaps the easiest to imitate is the eastern wolf. Because a human howl has exactly the same qualities as a wolf's call, wild wolves readily answer a human imitation. Nothing is more rewarding than to be under a star-studded sky and have a wolf's spine-tingling howl shatter the silence in response to your rendition of its call. Try giving a long howl that rises in the middle and drops at the end. Wait 10 to 15 seconds after an attempt before repeating it. I have found that if wolves are going to respond, it is usually after the second attempt. Sometimes, however, it takes several individual howls followed by

Moose take to the shallow waters in the summer to feast on water-shield and other aquatic plants.

When you look into the eyes of a wolf, you see the spirit of the wild.

several "group howls" (where one energetic person or a small group simulates a pack by giving several consecutive, partially overlapping howls each) to achieve a response. *Wolf Howling in Algonquin Provincial Park:* Algonquin Park Technical Bulletin No. 3 gives an excellent explanation of howling, and superb recordings of Algonquin wolves can be heard on the CD *Voices of Algonquin.*

Wolves will answer back at all times of day, so try howling any time, particularly if you find fresh

tracks or droppings (especially ones that are still steaming!). Night, however, is the best time to try, for sound carries better when the air is cool and there is less interference from wind, bird, leaf and traffic noise. Elevated sites adjacent to large openings such as creeks, lakes and bogs generally provide for better long-range transmission of sound and are the best places to try. I recommend that you avoid howling along Highway 60 on Thursdays in August, however. On those nights, the Park Interpretive Program offers Public Wolf Howls in which you can participate. (Please see the section on that activity in "The Highway 60 Corridor," page 87.)

Barred owls are common in Algonquin and can often be stimulated into calling by imitations of their booming "Who cooks for you, who cooks for you aawwwll." Other loud noises, including wolf howls, may also arouse a response, so don't think that you have an inferior voice if a barred owl responds to your wolf howl! *Voices of Algonquin* has superb recordings of this bird. It is noteworthy that in the daytime imitations or recordings of this call can attract a variety of birds, particularly woodpeckers such as yellow-bellied sapsuckers, northern flickers and the much sought-after black-backed woodpecker. Before using a playback, please read this chapter's section "Wildlife-viewing Etiquette" (page 50).

River otters are commonly seen cavorting along Algonquin waterways, noisily huffing and snorting or giving bird-like chirps. They can frequently be lured closer by imitations of their snorts. By blowing air through your mouth with your lips loosely flapping, you can produce an excellent rendition of an otter alarm call, and this sound inevitably piques their curiosity.

The tremendous opportunity to view wild animals is indisputably one of the very special features of Algonquin Park. Whether it is a chipmunk dominating a campground meal or an eastern wolf howling into the night, animals epitomize the untamed milieu for which the Park is famous. Please ensure that your enjoyment of these creatures does not have a detrimental effect either on them or on Algonquin.

Pine martens, tree-climbing weasels, are easily attracted by "squeaking."

TRACKS AND SCATS OF ALGONQUIN'S LARGE MAMMALS

summer   winter

MOOSE

winter

WHITE-TAILED DEER

EASTERN WOLF

after eating berries

after eating more solid food

BLACK BEAR

THE NATURE OF MOOSE

Even if you have never seen one, you likely know what a moose looks like, for, like an elephant, tiger or gorilla, it is one of those animals whose image is indelibly stamped on our minds. While its relatives the elk and the caribou also sport majestic antlers, the moose's long snout and its bell, the odd flap of skin that dangles under its chin, give it a unique appearance. Algonquin, with its healthy population of moose, is one of the best spots in the world to see one of these stately beasts.

Moose are the giants of Algonquin, standing 2 metres (6.5 feet) high at the shoulder and weighing up to 600 kg (1,300 lb). They are very active at night, and their habit of sauntering across the highway unfortunately results in a number of collisions with vehicles each year. Drive with great care, especially after sunset, and pay particular attention in areas marked with signs indicating high levels of moose activity. By no coincidence, these areas are also marked with the black streaks of skidding tires.

Antlers are grown anew each year, starting from rather humble beginnings.

Skid marks also identify good moose-viewing sites in spring and early summer when moose frequent roadside ditches in their annual search for sodium, a nutrient essential for their diet. They glean this from the water and mud where the residues of salt (alias sodium chloride) used to clear the pavement of snow during the winter have accumulated. On a good day you can see a half a dozen or more moose along the edges of Highway 60. However, because of hair loss due to natural moult and to winter ticks (moose rub and bite their hides to rid themselves of these natural parasites), they are not at their photogenic best in the spring. Wait until mid-summer when they are sporting their sleek summer coats and are finding sodium in the leaves and stems of water-shield and other aquatic plants in beaver ponds and lake shallows. In summer it is rare to complete a canoe trip in the Park Interior and not come across at least one of these magnificent animals.

For most of the year, bull moose are solitary creatures. Cows, on the other hand, stay with their calves for one full year. In years when food is plentiful, the winter has been kind, and the population is not overcrowded, most cows give birth to twins; in other years they produce only one calf. As is the case with most mammals, the males take no part in the upbringing of the young, and so family groups do not exist. Only in the mating season, the rut, might you see a bull associating with a cow and her calves, and even these associations last just a few days.

By mid-May cows head for birthing sites, abandoning their yearlings along the way. In Algonquin, islands and peninsulas are preferred sites, and canoeists occasionally encounter females and their young on them. Cows with newly born calves can be aggressive, so never approach them.

When the maples begin to flame with autumn colour, moose begin to burn with desire. The rut starts in mid-September and continues into early October. A bull's majestic antlers reach their maximum growth by the end of August, and their plush covering of skin, "velvet," is shed around the same time. By the start of the rut these bony head ornaments are at their finest. It may come as some surprise that antlers are primarily for show and not for fighting. They are important indicators of a bull's health and status, and cows may choose a mate in part by how impressive his antlers are. Between December and the end of January, long after the rut has ended, the antlers are shed. They are grown anew, and often more impressive, the following summer.

During the rut moose become quite vocal. The cows utter long, noisy bawls to attract bulls, which respond with a guttural "gawunk." Bulls also make noise with their headgear. To demonstrate their prowess to desiring cows and perhaps to rivals, bulls thrash their antlers against small saplings, often smashing them to bits. An explosive cracking of branches inevitably heralds the arrival of one of these gigantic beasts.

At dawn bulls can be lured into view by imitating a female's love call. This is done by pinching your nose, cupping your hands around your mouth with your thumbs under your chin, and uttering a long moan that drops off the end in a grunt. If you decide to try your hand at moose calling, be sure to be near some form of safe haven, such as your car. If a bull responds and saunters into view, stop calling, make no noise and avoid breaking sticks. Never lure a moose

across a road. Whether you call or not, if at any time you encounter a bull during the mating season be sure to give it plenty of space. They can be very aggressive animals when blinded by love.

A great bull moose swaggering through the dawn mist, its massive rack of antlers swaying from side to side, and glowing orange as it catches the first rays of sunlight, is awe-inspiring. Algonquin Park just happens to be one of the very best places to experience this sight, one of the most unforgettable in all of nature.

Moose will go underwater, and reputedly even dive, to obtain a snack of sodium.

Bulls take interest in cows only during their breeding season, the rut. This cow is lying down while her successful suitor stands guard.

THE NATURE OF WOLVES

Algonquin is world famous for its wolves because more people have encountered wolves in the Park than anywhere else on this planet. The encounter is mostly of an audible nature, for wolves are highly vocal and their deep haunting howls carry far into the night, particularly when they howl from a lakeside hill. Many canoeists meet wolves in this fashion during a canoe trip in the Park's vast Interior. Most of all, the wolf's fame arises from the ever-popular Public Wolf Howls that take place every August in Algonquin. On these events, after attending a program on wolves at the Outdoor Theatre, participants are taken to hear wild wolves answer back to the naturalist howlers.

When I began to work in Algonquin, the wolves were thought to be a small race of timber or gray wolves. This was still the thinking at the time I wrote *Howls of August*. However, in the late 1990s DNA analysis revealed a very different situation. Algonquin wolves were found to have DNA virtually identical to that of the endangered red wolves of the southeastern United States, not the gray wolves found farther north. This revolutionary discovery led to a compelling new portrait of the Park's most famous animal.

The reddish ears and flanks of Algonquin wolves reflect their genetic relationship with red wolves of the southern United States.

Algonquin wolves are now believed to be the remnants of a wolf population that once ranged across eastern North America. Colonization and the ensuing habitat change resulted in the population being not only largely decimated but also split into a northern and a southern fragment. Today, the southern population consists of red wolves, which now hover on the verge of extinction. The northern population, which includes Algonquin wolves, is now deemed to be a unique species recently named the "eastern wolf" (*Canis lycaon*).

Algonquin wolves may be small – males

average only around 28 kg (61 lb), females 3 kg (7 lb) lighter – but they are colourful, with rusty red ears, shoulders and flanks. Like other wolves, eastern wolves travel in packs through the entire year in relatively defined territories, although in winter, their territorial boundaries can fade. Particularly in the eastern part of Algonquin, wolves often migrate from the Park, following white-tailed deer, their favourite prey, to their wintering areas.

Each pack, which has seven members on average, is led by a dominant pair that produces a set of pups in late spring, in a den often dug on a hillside. By mid-July the pups outgrow their birth homes and are led to more spacious outdoor summer retreats. Beaver meadows and bog edges are often used as rendezvous sites (so named because when the adults return from hunting they meet, or rendezvous, with the pups at these sites). An open meadow-like habitat, shade and nearby water seem to be the essential elements of all rendezvous sites. At these sites the pups play and learn basic hunting skills at the expense of frogs and grasshoppers. They also learn to use their voices, which they do on a frequent basis.

When a Public Wolf Howl is held, it is almost always because a rendezvous site has been located within earshot of the road. Incidentally, the Public Howls occur in Algonquin on Thursdays in August only if wolves have been located. In recent years I have been conducting a Public Wolf Howl for Bonnechere Provincial Park. Although the talk is given in Bonnechere Park, the actual Howl takes place in Algonquin along the Basin Road.

The howls of wolves are their most important form of long-range communication. When we howl and simulate a wolf, our voices are so similar to theirs that the wolves believe they are hearing another wolf, and that is why they answer back. Pups are the least discriminating of all and readily respond to a human howl. Because adult wolves use howls to announce territorial ownership, they often do more than howl back. I have learned that if I wait patiently and quietly at the spot I howled from, after several minutes a wolf often arrives at the scene to investigate the brazen intruder. (Please see page 53 for more tips on howling for wolves.)

Do Algonquin wolves pose any risk to us? At one time I would have answered unequivocally "no!" for back then attacks were unknown. However, in recent years there have been a few

Wolves readily reply to human imitations of their howls

incidents. In almost every case, the animal had been known for some time to be unafraid of people, and in many cases had been fed. After a long period of associating with humans, some of these wolves eventually did attack, and children were the primary targets. Now, please don't think I am suggesting that wolves are dangerous and that you and your family's lives are in danger once you set foot in Algonquin. That is certainly not the case. Attacks by wolves have been few and far between. I suspect that it is a logical progression for a few wolves to lose their fear of humans, as for many generations they have not experienced the snares, guns and poison that were formerly used against them, even inside the Park, right up to the late 1950s. In the past half-century there have been countless thousands of wolf-human encounters (mostly unnoticed by the human elements) in which no aggression was shown to the wolves. Thus, it seems inevitable that a wolf that lacked fear of humans would appear in the population. If it experienced extensive contact with humans without repercussion, it could possibly proceed to the next, exceedingly rare, step. The wolf might see if a human was good to eat.

With the knowledge that a fearless wolf can pose a risk to humans, the Park has instigated the policy that a bold wolf is to be immediately discouraged. This is accomplished by using loud noises to frighten the wolf and by shooting it with rubber bullets. If, after a couple of bouts of "discouragement" the animal persists in approaching people, it will be destroyed. With this new policy in place, the possibility of meeting a bold wolf in Algonquin is more remote than ever.

The wolves of Algonquin have been well studied. Doug Pimlott and his crew performed the first major study, from 1958 to 1965. This was followed by years of research conducted by John Theberge of Waterloo University. Currently, Brent Patterson of the Ontario Ministry of Natural Resources is working with these fascinating animals. If you see a wolf wearing a belt around its neck, you are seeing a wolf that has been equipped with a radio transmitter so that more can be learned about its movements. If you are interested in finding out about the current research on wolves and other park animals, visit the Research link on the Park's website (www.algonquinpark.on.ca).

I have spent much time tracking and observing wolves and must say that they have given me no real cause to fear them but plenty of reason to respect them. They travel across difficult terrain through all manner of challenging weather. They maintain a strong social hierarchy within the pack, and hunt cooperatively to bring down large prey like deer and moose. Wolves are model parents, and the entire pack helps to rear the dominant pair's pups. Most of all, wolves are a quintessential part of the untamed spirit that envelops us when we visit Algonquin, and their wild voices touch our feelings in a most primal way.

Radio telemetry allows researchers to follow the movements of elusive creatures such as wolves.

THE NATURE OF BEARS

Few creatures worry people more than bears do. When one considers that most black bears in Algonquin weigh less than the average two-legged visitor, and are usually very shy creatures that vanish long before they are seen, this might seem a bit difficult to understand. Yet, black bears have the reputation of being dangerous and they seem to inspire fear. Why is that?

I believe there are several reasons. One is that bears are big and black and often active at night. Another is that bears are omnivores and therefore eat meat, including moose calves. A third is the portrayal of bears in sportsman magazines and Hollywood movies as being horrific man-eating creatures. Also, bears do occasionally wander through campsites and exploit food not safely packed away. And on exceedingly rare occasions, black bears attack humans.

Let me deal with the last reason first. In Algonquin, there have been a few isolated cases in which bears have attacked and even killed people. In each case, the bear was not hungry; nor was it a bear that was accustomed to acquiring food from human sources, such as dumps. Nor was the bear a female protecting her cubs. It seems that in

Although common in Algonquin, bears are not easy to see because of their shyness.

these *exceedingly* rare cases it was a healthy adult male bear that was looking to try a new type of food.

To understand how small the chances of meeting such a bear in Algonquin Park are, look at my experiences with bears. I have spent more time in the Park alone, often in remote regions many miles from the next human, and often at night, than most people have or ever will. I have encountered a surprisingly low number of bears and never once was I attacked or shown real aggression. On one occasion a female gave me a "bluff charge" when I was between her and her cubs. She ran at me, huffing and with teeth chomping. As I quickly backed away, she immediately moved to the cubs and vanished into the forest, with them following close behind. On the few other occasions when I have been close to females with cubs, either they all ran away or the cubs were sent scampering up a tree while mom sped off.

Today there are a couple of things that visitors can do to ensure they do not have a bad bear experience on an outing. Some wear "bear bells" that hang on a belt and clang as the wearer walks. Others carry a canister of "bear spray," pepper spray that can be shot into the face of an attacking creature. On my excursions I carry neither. Bells scare away not only bears but anything else with ears, including weasels, moose and other animals I hope to see. Bells also detract from the enjoyment of anyone else within earshot. I don't carry a can of spray for two reasons. I am already burdened with camera gear, binoculars and other naturalist paraphernalia. And I don't perceive the risk of meeting a bold bear high enough to warrant the expense and inconvenience. The risk of incurring injury while driving to the Park or of being struck by lightning are both magnitudes higher than the risk of being attacked by a bear. However, you must do what

makes you feel at ease in the woods. If you want some sort of extra protection, I recommend you carry a can of pepper spray and avoid the noisy bell option.

Enough said about the risk of an attack. Black bears are fascinating animals that are for the most part solitary creatures. They often wander great distances to find food, which varies dramatically through the seasons. In summer they turn over logs and pull them apart in search of insect grubs, and they dig up yellowjacket wasp nests in the ground. In late summer, they eat ripe berries, being particularly fond of blueberries, elderberries and pin cherries. In the autumn they climb red oaks for their acorns and they scale American beeches to devour their nuts. In early spring they graze on fresh grasses and sedges, and some catch spawning suckers. A bit later, when moose calves and white-tailed deer fawns are born, they eat fresh meat. Because of this seasonally varied diet, bear droppings change appearance at different times of the year. I find their late summer droppings the most attractive, for the high moisture content of the fruit gives them a loose, whorled appearance and they are stained with the colour of the berries. The seeds, which pass through the intestinal tract undamaged, add a nice finishing touch. With their form, colour, and texture, these scats remind me of an ice cream sundae. More important, they are evidence of how masterful and ingenious plants are when it comes to getting their seeds dispersed.

Mating occurs in mid-summer and during this time male black bears mark trees. They often use spruce trees for this purpose, perhaps because the gum that oozes from those trees better retains their scent. When scent marking, bears scratch a tree with their claws and then rub their backs against the bark, often while standing upright. A suitably impressed female mates with a male but does not maintain any form of long-term

association with him. Females spend winters alone and give birth in their dens, which are often under the roots or trunks of overturned trees, or in the hollow bases of a large trees. Some bears just lie down in a hollow and let the snow cover them. During their winter dormancy (which is not true hibernation for the body temperature stays near normal and only the heart rate drops), bears awaken easily and occasionally wander out of the den in exceptionally warm weather or when the den gets flooded by melting snow or heavy rain. The cubs stay with their mother for two years, spending their second winter snuggled up against their mom in her den.

Many black bears in Algonquin weigh little more than 68 kg (150 lb) and look more like large dogs than bears when they run away. At

time of writing, research is being conducted to learn more about their biology in Algonquin. Visit the Research link on the Park website (www.algonquinpark.on.ca) for current information on the status of research on this species.

Black bears are most easily viewed in Algonquin during the berry season in open locations where fruit-bearing plants grow. At this time a quiet visit (that means no bear bells!) to a good patch of blueberries at dawn or in the late evening can offer a prolonged view of these fascinating and much maligned animals.

This black bear is eating grass or sedge, not smoking it!

THE NATURE OF BEAVERS

If I were asked to name the most powerful animal in the Park, it would not be the moose or the eastern wolf. Nor would it be the black bear. The animal to get my nod of approval would be a quiet, rotund rodent called the beaver. Why? Well, beavers have the power to fell towering trees and transform flowing streams into placid ponds. And by creating their own habitat, they enable myriad other living things ranging in size from microscopic water fleas to mighty moose to survive in Algonquin Park.

While you might not see a beaver if your visit does not include a late evening or dawn outing, you will certainly see their signs. Beaver ponds and lakes inhabited by beavers are ubiquitous in Algonquin and, thus, so is one of their distinctive structures, the lodge. Since many of Algonquin's beavers build their lodges along the shore, do not always expect to see one in the middle of the pond, surrounded by water. Regardless of location, a beaver lodge is more than just a home; it is also an impenetrable fortress. Once inside, beavers are safe from all wolves and bears, their main predators; the only way into the lodge is through one of the underwater entrances. Contrary to earlier thinking, river otters pose virtually no threat to beavers.

A lodge is a large mound of sticks with a hollowed-out interior containing two levels. The upper level, furnished with a mat of shredded bark, is used for sleeping, while the lower one is used for eating and grooming. In the autumn the lodge receives a generous coating of mud, which seals off the inside of the lodge from the outside air, thus serving as insulation. To allow the beavers inside the lodge to breathe during the winter, a small area on the very top of the lodge is kept mud-free so that it can act as an air vent.

Beavers are active year-round and do not hibernate. They are strict vegetarians and eat the bark of certain trees, trembling aspen being their favourite. They also eat a lot of herbaceous material, including raspberry canes and leaves, bracken ferns, and fresh grasses and sedges. They will graze on the land but take most of their meals into the water, where they dine in safety. Beavers also eat a lot of water plants. The floating leaves of water-shield, and the leaves, stems and roots of water-lilies, especially bullhead-lily, are important components of most beavers' diets. In winter they eat the roots of water plants, but the main item on most beavers' winter menu is tree bark. They acquire the bark not by venturing onto land but by retrieving branches from a large stockpile

Beavers use their tails to help keep them afloat as they dine on the roots and stems of water plants.

they have built in the water next to the lodge. This winter larder, known as the "food pile," is created in the fall and is accessed from under the ice. Thus, in winter a beaver can exit its lodge and return with a branch without ever being detected by human eyes or even leaving a sign.

In addition to the lodge, many beavers build a second structure, one that is familiar to most canoeists. Beaver dams stop the flow in many an Algonquin stream, creating ponds deep enough not to freeze to the bottom in winter. The latticework masterpieces they create are responsible for providing one of the most important and intriguing habitats in Algonquin Park. Beavers inspect their dams regularly for leaks, which they detect by ear. They use mud, sticks – and even stones – to plug up breaks. After heavy rains, look for beavers performing maintenance work on their dams in the evening or at dawn.

Beavers are primarily creatures of the night and thus are seldom seen in daytime. They do, however, venture out of the lodge during daylight hours on heavily overcast days, and frequently start dining an hour or so before sunset. One of the best ways to find beavers is to look in early evening among the leaves of water-lilies for their heads sticking up amongst them. They are also very easily found by surveying calm lake surfaces at sunset or sunrise. A "V" wake cutting across the surface is a sure sign of a beaver heading out in search of food or returning to its lodge for a well-deserved sleep.

The large blunt head of the beaver is distinctive. Unlike those of most mammals, the beaver's ears, eyes and nose are lined up in a neat row so that these sensory tools are all above water

when they swim. The nose and ears contain valves that close when a beaver dives, and the eyes have a transparent membrane that acts like diving goggles. When a beaver dives it can mysteriously vanish. Internal adaptations, including an oversized liver, allow it to stay underwater for up to 15 minutes!

Beavers' large hind feet are fully webbed and serve to propel them through the water. While they are excellent swimmers, beavers will never set any speed records. Their body plan is a compromise for swimming and for walking on land as well as for towing heavy loads both into and out of the water. One of their primary adaptations for this unusual life style is their large flat, scaly tail – one of the most specialized tools in the animal kingdom. It is used as a rudder for swimming. It serves as a brace when a beaver is sitting up to groom or to fell a tree. It is a storage chamber for fat used as fuel in winter. It functions as an air conditioner in summer when additional warm blood is pumped through it. And it is an essential tool for communication. The explosive crack of a beaver's tail slapped across the water's surface not only startles the cause of distress but also warns other colony members of danger.

Beavers are truly remarkable animals. Their stick blockades that transform flowing stream into quiet ponds, their noisy tail slaps that waken the night, and their distinctive wakes that slowly dissect calm evening lakes are every bit a piece of Algonquin as the mournful wails of loons and the mists of dawn.

A coat of fresh mud and a burgeoning food pile indicate that this lodge is actively housing beavers.

The bark of the trembling aspen is one of the beaver's favourite foods.

THE NATURE OF LOONS

Few sounds evoke images of the wild more than the calls of a common loon. These beautiful birds inhabit all but the smallest lakes in Algonquin, and most large lakes host two or more pairs. Loons are masters of the water, diving and swimming with the agility of otters. Their speed underwater allows them to catch even the fastest of fish, and their diet seldom varies.

Because loons are birds of the water, canoeists frequently meet up with them. Not uncommonly a loon will emerge right beside a canoe, silver drops of water beading down its head and back, uttering a soft laugh-like call. However, loon's nest can be quite difficult to see as they are usually built in secluded locations. Loons usually nest along the shores of quiet bays and islands, on top of mounds of mud and vegetation. Even when a loon is sitting on its eggs, the nest is hard to find; when disturbed, an incubating loon squats down with its bill close to the water, its white necklace and back spots creating the perfect camouflage for a sun-dappled shoreline.

Common loons usually have two chicks, but occasionally produce only one.

Both members of the pair take turns incubating the usual two eggs, which hatch in 29 days. Within an hour of hatching, the dark fuzz-ball chicks abandon the nest and swim with their parents, which feed them tiny fish. Loons chicks often get free rides, nestled on their parents' backs.

Loons propel themselves underwater with their large webbed hind feet, which for maximum thrust are set very close to the tail-less back end. This same feature makes it very difficult for them to walk when out of water. Their ability to stay submerged for a minute or even longer allows loons to perform great vanishing acts as well as mysterious reappearances.

Because they are devoted parents and interact so peacefully with humans, common loons have often been described as gentle birds. Yet there is another side to loons that is shown during territorial intrusions either by loons or by other fish-eating competitors. I once watched a loon quietly swim with head barely above water toward an unsuspecting female common merganser. Then it dove, only to suddenly reappear shooting up through water from right beneath the startled duck, its bill pointed to the sky like an arrow shot out of an underwater bow.

There are scattered records of loons killing their "fish duck" competitors and also of loons killing loons. I once witnessed the latter phenomenon outside of Algonquin. Two loons, presumably males, battled fiercely, deploying their wings as clubs to whack their opponent across the head and neck. They grappled with each other, using their bills as spears. One received a serious chest wound that coloured its white breast red whenever it reared up in the water. The other fared even more poorly. It appeared to be speared through the neck and every time the dominating bird's wing hit its neck, blood shot out of its wound and from its open mouth. As it weakened, it was held underwater in an apparent attempt to drown it. After a few fruitless attempts to break free and escape, it surfaced no more. I was very fortunate to record this remarkable and savage fight on video.

Although many dead loons with healed chest wounds have been found, fights of this nature are rarely witnessed. In Algonquin you are most apt to see dramatic raised-wing displays and wild chases across the water. And you will most certainly hear the vocalizations they use to intimidate intruding birds and to communicate with their mates and chicks.

Loons have at least four distinct sounds. The tremolo is the laugh-like call given to express distress, often uttered when canoeists approach a nest. The wail is the wolf-like call that fools many visitors into thinking they are hearing a mammal and not a bird. Yodels, the wildest songs of all, combine melodious rising and falling notes with flippant endings. When two or more loons join the chorus, the night is awakened by the wild cacophany. The CD *Voices of Algonquin* contains wonderful recordings of loon music accompanied by narration that explains the context of the different songs and the soft "hoot" that is heard in family groups.

Loons arrive in Algonquin shortly after the ice is off the lakes, which is usually around the first of May, and stay until about a month before December's freeze-up. Most loons winter in the Atlantic Ocean, where they dine on a diet of salt-water fish while dressed in a drab coat of grey and white. Fortunately for park visitors, they don their distinctive coat of glossy green-black and speckled black-and-white before they return.

Their belligerent side notwithstanding, common loons are to Algonquin as a piano was to Beethoven. They give voice to the Park in a uniquely wild and beautiful way.

A loon's nest, consisting of a push-up of mud and plant debris, is always in or next to water.

Although loons also carry their chicks on their back, they never have as many to transport as this female common merganser does.

SEASONAL HIGHLIGHTS

Every season brings a new palette and dramatic changes to Algonquin. Both the landscape and the wildlife undergo spectacular transformations in the course of a year. Many of the phenomena for which the Park is famous demonstrate seasonal peaks in either activity or occurrence. By knowing the times of the year in which they occur, one can better plan a trip to coincide with some of those particular highlights (or, in the case of biting insects, to avoid them). The Algonquin Park website (www.algonquinpark.on.ca) provides up-to-date information.

Each month is broken into three periods – early, middle and late. You might find that the symbol for "fair" activity (◇) is indicated for the first of the month, the symbol for a higher level of activity, (◆) for "good," in the middle of the month, and the symbol representing the highest level of activity, (▲) for "high," at the end of the month. This simply indicates that your best chance of encountering a particular animal or phenomenon lies at the end of the month rather than the beginning.

The blooming period for park wildflowers lasts from mid-April to mid-September. However,

Visitors come to Algonquin from all over the world for the annual display of autumn colours.

different habitats produce distinct peaks in the flower cycles. In the hardwood forests the floor is carpeted with flowers from late April through to late May, the period when the forest floor is not yet shaded by overhead leaves. As soon as the canopy closes over, these ephemerals quickly vanish. A few shade-tolerant species, such as Indian pipe, bloom in the summer shade, and a large variety of flowers bloom in the summer along the roadsides and other open sites where sunlight is unimpeded. For a fascinating and highly visual overview of the various habitats and their dominant flowers, be sure to acquire *Wildflowers*

of Algonquin Provincial Park, an inexpensive Friends of Algonquin publication.

The peak of the famed fall leaf colour varies in both timing and intensity from year to year. Generally, the last week of September and the first week of October display the best colours in the sugar maples. However, by the time the maples are finishing their show, other trees are coming into colour. Poplars are the next to turn, and their colour is a deep yellow. The view from the Visitor Centre opens onto spectacular displays of these trees. As time passes, the red oaks turn reddish-brown and can be seen on hilltops throughout the Park, particularly in the East Side. Last, but not least, are the tamaracks, or larches. These bog-loving trees are the only coniferous trees to drop their needles, but just before the needles fall, they turn an intense gold. Waterways all through the Park blaze with tamarack gold in the latter part of

SEASONAL OCCURRENCES OF A FEW ALGONQUIN PHENOMENA

SUBJECT OF INTEREST	JAN.	FEB.	MAR.	APR.	MAY	JUNE	JULY	AUG.	SEPT.	OCT.	NOV.	DEC.
River Otters	◇◇◇	◇◇◇	◆◆▲	▲▲▲	◆◇◇	◇◇◇	◇◆◆	◆◆◆	◆◆◆	◆◆◆	◆◆◇	◇◇◇
Moose			◆◆▲	▲▲▲	▲▲▲	▲▲▲	▲▲▲	◆◆◆	◆◆◆	◆◆◆	◆◆◆	◇◇
Wildflowers				◇◆	▲▲◆	◆◆▲	▲▲▲	◆◆◇	◇◇			
Wolf Howling	◆◆◆	◆◆◆	◆◆◆	◆◇◇	◇◇◇	◇◇◇	◆◆▲	▲▲▲	▲▲▲	▲▲◆	◆◆◆	◆◆◆
Beavers			◇◆▲	▲▲▲	▲▲▲	▲▲▲	▲▲▲	▲▲▲	▲▲▲	▲▲▲	◆◇	
Biting Insects				◇◇	◇◆▲	▲▲▲	▲◆◆	◇◇				
Fall Colours									◇◆▲	▲◆◇		
Snowshoeing / Cross Country Skiing	▲▲▲	▲▲▲	▲◆◇									◇◆▲
Common Loons				◇◆▲	▲▲▲	▲▲▲	▲▲▲	◆◇◇	◇			

Level of Activity ◇ FAIR ◆ GOOD ▲ HIGH

October and early November.

If you wish to see the peak of the colours, I recommend that you look at the Park website for current conditions and forecast peak times. You can also call the Park Information Services (705-633-5572) – but be prepared to wait, as the office is often hard to reach because of high demand.

As the snow conditions for cross country skiing vary from year to year, check the Park website or call for information on trail conditions, particularly if you plan to ski at either end of the season.

One seasonal feature of Algonquin not illustrated on the above chart is the Northern Lights. Because the Park is situated on a high dome with no interference from city lights, the night sky is deliciously dark. This darkness offers excellent stargazing opportunities and periodic views of the spectacular aurora borealis, the Northern Lights. The bizarre shimmering lights of the aurora are caused by interactions between the Earth's magnetic field and pockets of intensified magnetism in the sun's atmosphere. The aurora can be seen at virtually any time of the year but its appearance does vary greatly. Quite often it appears as a dull glow in the northern sky, while at other times it shoots out into the night in the form of pulsating rays. Occasionally, strong colours are present, with green being frequent and red less common. At times, vivid rays fill the entire sky in a cathedral effect, creating a rare display that simply carries you away.

The timing of the peak of the fall colour can vary by as much as two to three weeks from year to year.

Winter is a great time for all ages to explore new parts of Algonquin, such as the roofs of beaver lodges!

SOME COMMON ALGONQUIN CONIFERS

BALSAM FIR

WHITE SPRUCE

BLACK SPRUCE

TAMARACK

EASTERN WHITE CEDAR

EASTERN HEMLOCK

JACK PINE

RED PINE

WHITE PINE

LEAVES OF SELECT ALGONQUIN DECIDUOUS TREES

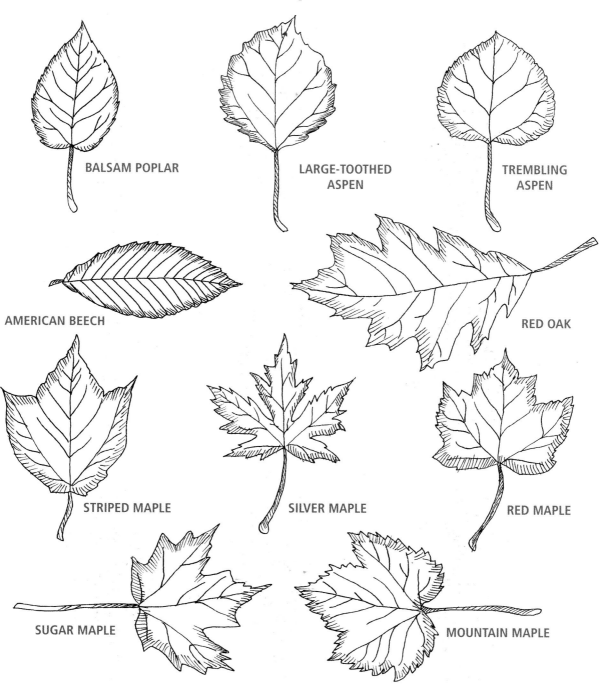

BALSAM POPLAR

LARGE-TOOTHED ASPEN

TREMBLING ASPEN

AMERICAN BEECH

RED OAK

STRIPED MAPLE

SILVER MAPLE

RED MAPLE

SUGAR MAPLE

MOUNTAIN MAPLE

HIGHLIGHTS TO AVOID

Biting Insects

The main challenge to camping in Algonquin, or even visiting the Park at certain times of the year, is dealing with the biting insects. The good news is that each type of biting fly has its own particular season. The bad news is that the seasons tend to merge together, producing a prolonged period of bloodletting. However, each person responds to each type of fly differently, and there are ways of reducing your attractiveness to these biting terrors.

First, let's meet the little devils. The black fly is one of the smallest biting flies in Algonquin, yet it is the most infamous. As black flies lay their eggs on rocks in fast-flowing, cold streams, Algonquin is just perfect for them. The majority emerge as adults from these cold waters usually between mid-May and mid-June. However, in an early spring they might venture out in late April, and in some years they persist well into July.

When you first meet black flies, you will be amazed at how such tiny creatures can make life so miserable. Black flies are active on warm days, particularly in the evening, but they desist after sunset. As with other biting flies, only the female bites, seeking a blood meal for her developing eggs. However, black flies tend to tear flesh, rather than pierce it. Blood, induced by anti-coagulants injected into the wounds, flows copiously from the small gashes. Just like sharks drawn to a bloodbath, swarms of other black flies soon appear and a feeding frenzy quickly erupts. It is their numbers, not just their nip, that make this species intolerable to so many people.

Mosquitoes are the next most common type of biting fly in Algonquin. Although mosquitoes have a much longer flying season than black flies (they tend to appear by late May and some species remain active into the middle of August), they are rarely as bothersome as their smaller relatives. Of course, this is all very subjective; some people find a couple of mosquitoes totally unbearable. Mosquitoes tend to dominate the last hour or so of the day, but if you're prowling around moist woods, especially cedar swamps, be prepared to meet lots of them. Any portage through rich hardwoods or low areas will inevitably also attract a hungry swarm.

By midsummer, another "nasty" appears. The deer fly is a large fly with banded wings and gorgeous eyes (usually red or green). Deer flies love to buzz around your head, their most common point of attack, and when they bite, they impart a nasty burning prick. Their larger relative, the horse fly, inflicts an even more painful jab.

Another type of fly that might buzz you in summer, particularly along waterways, is the stable fly. These housefly-sized insects have the annoying habit of biting your ankles when you are canoeing and are very adept at escaping your swat no matter how fast you may be.

And there is yet one more. The "no-see-um," or biting midge, is almost invisible, but its tiny searing bite can make you utter very unpleasant words!

With all that said, what can you possibly do, apart from visiting the Park at another time of year … say, December? Well, there are actually a few things that can cut down on the annoyance that these small but at times dominant insects might cause you.

A number of effective insect repellents are

In the height of the season, hordes of mosquitoes wait under the fly of a tent for you to emerge.

available on the market. Since biting insects tend to be stimulated by water vapour gradients next to your skin, the drying effects of these repellents tend to disrupt insects' detection systems. Many types contain the active ingredient DEET. While these repellents work quite well for many people, I can't offer advice as to which types work better than others for the simple reason that I don't use them. I dislike the "melt down" effect most of the brands have on binoculars or camera equipment. Some types lack DEET in their constitution and use more pleasant components such as citronella.

"Deer Fly Patches" are sticky patches that attach to a hat. They look like a bald head ripe for harvesting and they entice deer flies to land on them. After a patch becomes filled with flies stuck by their feet, you replace the patch with a new one. Never having used these, I can't tell you how effective they are. However, I have heard they work quite well, with as many as 28 flies reportedly being caught on one patch.

Clothing selection is certainly important in insect avoidance. Many biting flies are attracted to dark colours, particularly navy blue and black. I will never forget paddling by a Tea Lake campsite one evening in early June. On the point stood a forlorn-looking woman, dressed in black pants, a black top and a black hat. This was at the height of the black fly season, and her face and neck were a mass of open bleeding wounds from fly bites. Although I was not enjoying the company of the flies swarming around me, I bore the marks of only a handful of bites on my exposed flesh. Lighter colours, such as pale yellow or light tan, are less attractive to these insects and, while not a perfect solution, do help you partically escape the full force of the biting masses.

Clothing should also be loose-fitting, with tight cuffs. I fasten all buttons and raise my collar. Often I wear a light-coloured, lightweight jacket over my shirt. A hat is essential for keeping pests out of your hair. Flies love tender ankles for dessert, so a pair of heavier socks pulled over your pant legs will give needed protection. I must admit this attire makes you look rather silly, but in the height of fly season in Algonquin, being fashion-wise is about as sensible as wearing high-heeled shoes on the Centennial Ridges Trail.

Another trick that I find quite successful is somewhat embarrassing to share with you. Perfumes in soaps and shampoos seem to attract insects, as do skin pores that are open from frequent bathing. If I am camping or taking photographs in peak fly season, I tend to bathe very irregularly. When I absolutely must wash, I avoid using soap. I am convinced that there is an inverse relationship between the number of flies that bite you and the number of days since your last shower. Also, I wear the same clothes for as long as possible without washing them. Although these are effective ways of reducing the number of biting flies around you, you won't likely win many friends.

There are some excellent bug-proof clothes on the market, including the traditional netted "bug hat," which makes you look like an extra on the X Files. Even better are "bug jackets" or "bug shirts," which keep insects away from your body. They have elasticized cuffs, a drawstring waist, and a hood with a mesh face guard that can be unzipped at the neck to free your head. The one I have (but admittedly seldom use) is "The Original Bug Shirt." It is made of lightweight cotton with vents to prevent sweating, and is a pale tan. In the ultimate test, I sat by a beaver pond for several hours one evening in the height of black fly season with this jacket on. I was amazed that none of the 2,989 black flies swarming outside this barrier were able to get in. I was also pleased that I could see well enough through the mesh to focus my camera without undoing the hood.

Whatever method you use to combat biting insects, there are always some inherent drawbacks. However, you will find that the more you expose yourself to bites, the less bothersome they become. If you are severely affected by bites, as some people are, I would recommend that you come to Algonquin during the off-season for flies. Usually the period from mid-August to late September lacks these friendly creatures, and at this time the temperatures are still quite pleasant for hiking, canoeing and sleeping in a tent.

Poisonous Snakes, Poison Ivy and Poison Mushrooms

Campers are frequently concerned about poisonous plants and animals. As noted earlier, there are no poisonous snakes in Algonquin. Garter snakes are the only common snakes in the Park. Northern water snakes, also harmless, are primarily found on the East Side only.

Apart from one tiny station near Tea Lake, there is no poison ivy along the Highway Corridor. More often than not, immature plants of sarsaparilla are misidentified as being this irritating plant. However, poison ivy is infrequently encountered north of the Highway 60 Corridor although it is relatively common along rivers in the eastern side of the Park, such as the very popular Barron River.

There are a few poisonous mushrooms, including several species of amanitas, in Algonquin, so unless you are extremely familiar with this group, avoid eating wild mushrooms during your visit. I recommend *Mushrooms of Algonquin Provincial Park* for those interested in learning more about this varied and essential group of organisms.

This mosquito is interested not in the columbine it is resting on but in blood carried by someone like you!

Poison ivy is almost exclusively an East Side plant and is confined primarily to the shores of certain rivers.

Massasauga rattlesnakes, not found in Algonquin, use poison to subdue their prey.

Discomfort along the Trails

As most of the Interpretive Trails are quite short, no special suggestions are needed for them, apart from wearing suitable footwear. However, a few trails, such as Mizzy Lake, are longer and require more time to complete. To avoid running into difficulty, I recommend setting out on the trail early in the morning. If you do start a longer trail later in the day, be sure to bring along a flashlight with functional batteries, some food, and some extra clothing in case it gets cool.

On any trail it is prudent to carry a small daypack with a bit of nourishment (such as trail-mix, chocolate or fruit) and some type of liquid (water is the best) in a container that will return with you. It can become quite hot in summer and most of the longer trails have hills.

It is also a good idea to bring along some toilet paper, for one never knows when nature will call. Be sure to be discreet if you participate in this activity. Walk well off the trail, deposit the "goods" in a depression and cover up the "dirty deed" with leaves and soil once you are finished. Never leave tissues strewn about for others to see.

Other Hazards of the Trail

At present, hunting occurs in two parts of Algonquin. In the southern townships of Clyde, Bruton and Eyre, this activity occurs in the fall. And members of the Algonquin First Nation hunt through much of the eastern half of Algonquin from mid-October through to mid-January or until they meet their quota. If you plan on canoeing or hiking through these parts of Algonquin during the season when hunting is allowed, I recommend that you wear bright orange clothing. Perhaps bear bells might be a wise item to wear, but in this case not necessarily for four-legged animals to hear!

For more information on hunting in Algonquin Park, contact Algonquin Park Information Services (705-633-5567) or visit the Algonquin Park website, www.algonquinpark.on.ca.

THE HIGHWAY 60 CORRIDOR

The most popular and most developed route into Algonquin Park is Highway 60. The majority of the Park's campgrounds, interpretive trails and facilities, as well as other services, are situated along what is known as the Highway 60 Corridor. Despite the developed aspect and prominent use of this part of Algonquin, it is still possible to feel as if you are really "back in the woods" and have a bona fide wilderness experience. Also, wildlife-viewing opportunities in the Corridor are equal to, in some cases better than, those off the road in the Park Interior.

Every vehicle that stops at a park facility must display a permit. These, as well as information, are available at both the East and West gates. Day passes and seasonal passes are both available. The information building at the East Gate is accessed from the right lane as you pass through a set of arches. The West Gate lies 4 km (2.5 miles) inside the actual west boundary of the Park (identified by a sign beside the road). Remember, you must have a permit whether you are in Algonquin for half a day or a week. Only drivers that pass through the Park without stopping at any of its facilities are exempt from purchasing a permit.

Reflective signs, frequently situated on telephone poles, indicate the distance in kilometres from the West Gate. In all Algonquin

Highway 60 takes you through stunning hardwood forests in the heart of the Western Highlands.

literature, locations of sites of interest are pinpointed using these kilometre markers. I use the same reference system in this book when describing locations along the Corridor.

The Western Uplands Backpacking Trail, for example, is located 3 km (1.9 miles) east of the West Gate at the KM 3 sign, and the road to the Algonquin Visitor Centre exits Highway 60 at the KM 43 marker, 43 km (26.7 miles) east of the West Gate. For more precise location descriptions, I include the distance between markers. The Mizzy Lake Trail entrance, for example, is situated 0.4 km east of the KM 15 marker. Thus, its location is given as KM 15.4.

As you reach the Park boundaries, you will see signs notifying you of the Park Information radio channel. By tuning in to CFOA at FM 102.7 on your car radio, you will receive a brief overview of current Park services and highway phenomena. Algonquin also offers a weather radio broadcast called Weatheradio. The broadcast, sent at 162,400 MHz, can only be picked up by Weatheradio receivers, which are available at many outfitting, electronic and marine stores. The Canadian Location Code (CLC) needed to set a receiver for Algonquin is 044300. See Environment Canada's Weatheradio Network, website, www.msc-smc.ec.ge.ca/msb/weatheradio/, for more information.

A useful summary of the current Corridor facilities and activities can be found in the free tabloid *Algonquin Information Guide* available at most park offices or upon request by mail or phone. Current information can also be found on the Algonquin Park website, www.algonquinpark.on.ca.

It is worth getting up early to catch a sunrise over Mew Lake, right beside Highway 60.

ALGONQUIN
PROVINCAL PARK

TORONTO ■

ONTARIO

DETAILED ACCESS MAPS

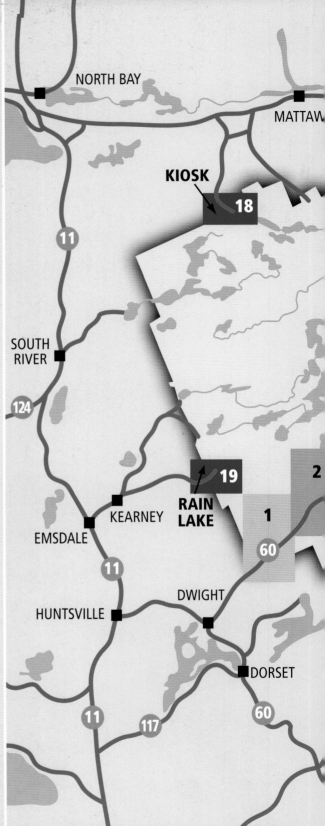

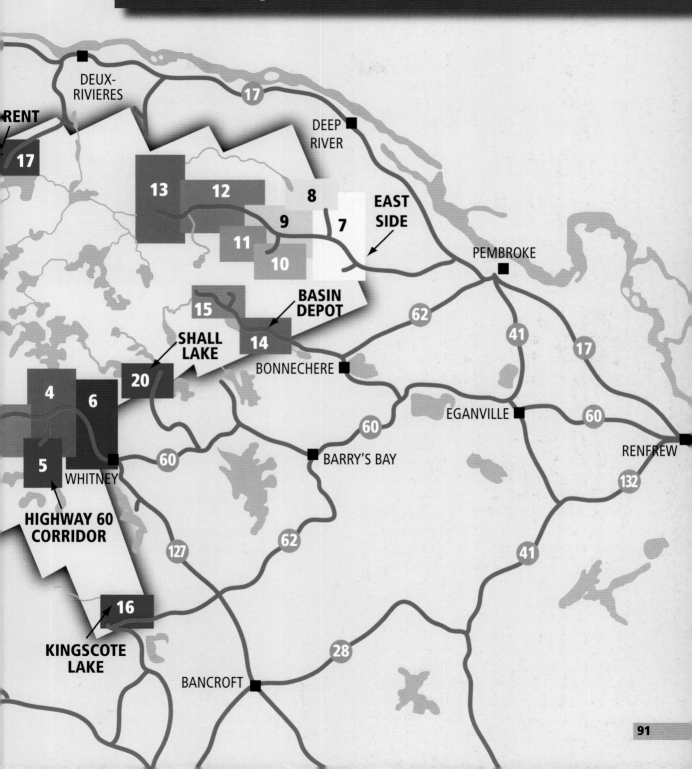

ACCESS POINTS TO ALGONQUIN PROVINCIAL PARK

DEUX-RIVIERES

17

DEEP RIVER

RENT

17

13

12

8

9

7

EAST SIDE

11

10

BASIN DEPOT

PEMBROKE

15

62

SHALL LAKE

14

41

17

20

BONNECHERE

4

6

60

EGANVILLE

60

5

60

BARRY'S BAY

RENFREW

WHITNEY

132

HIGHWAY 60 CORRIDOR

127

62

41

16

KINGSCOTE LAKE

28

BANCROFT

THE ALGONQUIN VISITOR CENTRE
KM 43

A major project undertaken for the Algonquin Park centennial in 1993, the Algonquin Visitor Centre is without question one of the finest interpretive centres in Canada. Every aspect of this showpiece, including its breathtaking location, is visitor-friendly.

The first section of the display area illustrates how the Park's topography has affected the present-day composition of flora and fauna through its influence on climate and soils. The next gallery features stunning dioramas of all the Park's major habitats, from spruce bog to hardwood forest, from lake to coniferous forest. The habitats and the animals that live in them, from tiny shrews to massive moose, are not only as lifelike as you can imagine (thanks to the world-class talent of diorama specialist Kevin Hockley) but are set against backdrops that are genuine works of art, all painted by renowned artist Dwayne Harty. Whether it be the beaver pond diorama complete with dam, pond, lodge and swimming beavers, or the black bear exhibit, in which a mother bear tears apart a log with one of her two small cubs looking on with curiosity, the realism is remarkable.

The level of the building devoted to human history profiles man's role in Algonquin. Its exhibits focus on the impact of people ranging from the earliest inhabitants to more recent residents, such as the famous artist Tom Thomson. A comfortable theatre offers programs that further explain the past and present features of Algonquin.

The dioramas, displays and programs have all been designed to present the complexity of Algonquin Park in such a way that visitors are better prepared to appreciate the "real thing," which is gloriously on display from a partially enclosed viewing deck. The deck offers a vista that

The Visitor Centre is perched on a hill offering a spectacular view of many park habitats.

encompasses a sweeping bog, rolling hardwood hills, part of a lake and a fringe of boreal forest – the very subjects explained through the displays inside. The view alone is worth the trip to the Visitor Centre. As an extra bonus, animals such as moose, black bears and eastern wolves can often be seen or heard from this phenomenal vantage point.

The Visitor Centre also contains a restaurant and one of the finest natural history bookstores anywhere, as well as the Algonquin Room, in which temporary art exhibits (for sale) are displayed.

The Visitor Centre is open seven days a week for most of the year except for the winter, when it is open just on weekends. In July and August the hours are 9 a.m. to 9 p.m. The Algonquin Park website, www.algonquinpark.on.ca, lists all hours and days of operation. Be sure to set aside part of a day – at the very least – to visit this outstanding facility.

MAP 1
HIGHWAY CORRIDOR KM 1– KM 9

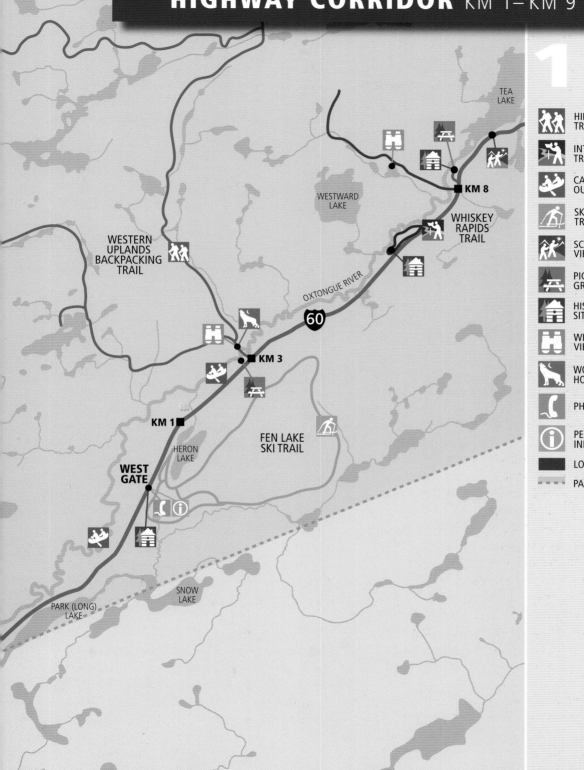

TEA LAKE

WESTWARD LAKE

KM 8

WHISKEY RAPIDS TRAIL

WESTERN UPLANDS BACKPACKING TRAIL

OXTONGUE RIVER

60

KM 3

KM 1

HERON LAKE

FEN LAKE SKI TRAIL

WEST GATE

SNOW LAKE

PARK (LONG) LAKE

1

	HIKING TRAIL
	INTERPRETIVE TRAIL
	CANOE OUTING
	SKI TRAIL
	SCENIC VIEW
	PICNIC GROUND
	HISTORIC SITE
	WILDLIFE VIEWING
	WOLF HOWLING
	PHONE
	PERMITS/ INFORMATION
	LOGGING ROAD
	PARK BOUNDARY

THE ALGONQUIN LOGGING MUSEUM KM 54.6

This outdoor museum offers a fascinating look at an important aspect of Algonquin's history. The log reception building houses an information desk, a bookstore, a theatre and dioramas that depict logging activities through the years. An audiovisual program gives an overview of the history of logging in the Park, and a delightful trail, complete with guidebook, starts from the reception building and leads through the outdoor exhibits. These

include a replica of an early "camboose camp" and one of the last remaining "alligators," a steam-driven paddleboat that could also be winched across land. Alligators, which towed log booms, were last used in the early twentieth century. Appropriately, this unique exhibit has been placed beside a scenic pond created by a replicated log dam. A log chute, similar to the ones used to slide logs around waterfalls and rapids, bypasses the small rapids below the dam.

The outdoor exhibits are strategically located along this trail in a chronological sequence, allowing visitors to follow the development of logging from a century and a half ago to the present. The Algonquin Logging Museum is open from late May until Thanksgiving weekend.

The *William M.* on the Logging Museum Trail is one of the last "alligators" still in existence.

THE ALGONQUIN ART CENTRE KM 20

Long-time park users will recognize the building as being the old Park Museum, which received visitors at this site from 1953 until 1992. It now houses art works and fine crafts (for display and sale), with one room dedicated to a specific theme, such as wolves. The Art Centre is open seasonally from 10 a.m. to 5:30 p.m., and access is free with a vehicle day pass or a seasonal pass. For more information, call 705-633-5555.

THE INTERPRETIVE WALKING TRAILS

One of the most attractive features of the Highway 60 Corridor is its variety of superb interpretive walking trails. There are 14 distinctly different trails, each offering unique insights into the Park's habitats and fascinating history. An inexpensive ($0.37 in 2007!) illustrated trail guide booklet is available at the start of each trail or at retail outlets in the Park. Each booklet contains text with numbered sections designed to be read at the appropriate posts along each trail, allowing you to learn first hand and at your leisure about Algonquin's many facets.

Here is a brief synopsis of the different trails along the Highway Corridor, starting from the west. The trail's location along the highway appears beside its name, and its length appears after the trail description.

- **Whiskey Rapids Trail** KM 7.2
  This trail follows the scenic Oxtongue River, and the trail guide booklet explores the ecology of an Algonquin river. If you wade into the top of the shallow rapid, look for the bright green lumps of freshwater sponges

and the trumpet-shaped nets of net-spinning caddisflies. At the rapids watch for a fast-flying yellow and black dragonfly sporting a large "club," or swelling, at the end of its abdomen. If huge, it is likely the dragonhunter, and if medium-sized, the zebra clubtail, a fast-water species. The trail's name is derived from a story that involves a spilled keg of whiskey. (2.1 km/1.3 miles)

■ **Hardwood Lookout Trail** KM 13.8
This short trail leads you through a beautiful hardwood forest, and the trail guide booklet explores its ecology. Scenic views of the Smoke Lake area and a side trail to a stand of red spruce, a rare tree in Algonquin, are splendid highlights. (0.8 km/0.5 mile)

■ **Mizzy Lake Trail** KM 15.4
This, the second-longest of the Corridor trails, is well worth the effort, for it passes through some outstanding wildlife-viewing areas, particularly in the northern part. The trail visits a total of nine small lakes and ponds, and the wildlife they support is highlighted in the trail guide. In the ponds at the north end of the trail, which follows the historic Ottawa, Arnprior & Parry Sound (OA&PS) Railway bed at this point, look for turtles with numbers on their shells (they are the subjects of a long-term research project). This is also an excellent place to hear wolves and see otters. Because of the abundance of wild animals, dogs are not allowed on this trail. (7.7 km/4.8 miles)

■ **Peck Lake Trail** KM 19.2
The ecology of a very pretty lake, Peck Lake, is the focus of this trail, which meanders around the lake periphery through a delightful coniferous forest. (1.9 km/1.2 miles)

■ **Track and Tower Trail** KM 25
This popular trail explores some of the fascinating history of Algonquin. It travels through extensive hardwood forests and crosses several pretty streams. The historic sites include remnants of several trestles of the OA&PS Railway and the site of a former fire lookout tower with a spectacular view over Cache Lake. Part of the trail lies on the old rail bed of the OA&PS Railway. The Track and Tower Trail can also be accessed from Mew Lake. (7.7 km/4.8 miles with an optional 5.5 km/3.4-mile loop from Mew Lake)

■ **Hemlock Bluff Trail** KM 27.2
This trail first leads through a grove of towering eastern hemlocks and later visits a cliff overlooking Jack Lake. Research in Algonquin is the topic examined in the trail guide booklet. Barred owls often call from the hemlocks in the late afternoon or early morning. (3.5 km/2.2 miles)

■ **Bat Lake Trail** KM 30
This trail is relatively easy to walk despite its length. It passes through a younger mixed forest, enters an exceptionally large hemlock grove, traverses a bog and visits a fine lookout as well as a naturally acidified lake. The trail guide booklet examines basic ecological principles. (5.6 km/3.5 miles)

■ **Two Rivers Trail** KM 31
A fine view from a cliff top is the highlight of this trail, which wanders through a younger Algonquin forest. The trail guide booklet explores the dynamics of forest change. (2.1 km/1.3 miles)

- **Centennial Ridges Trail** 2 km (1.2 miles) south from KM 37.6
  This trail gets its name from its year of opening – 1993, which was the Algonquin Park centennial. It is the most rugged of all the Highway Corridor trails, but you'll know that the physical effort was worth it when you reach the top of two ridges visited by the trail and gaze out over some of the finest views in Algonquin. It is a very good trail for encountering wildlife, including black bears when they are feeding on blueberries in late summer. The trail guide booklet details contributions made by famous Algonquin personalities. (10 km/6 miles)

- **Lookout Trail** KM 39.7
  One of the most enjoyable of all the Algonquin trails, Lookout Trail holds true to its name by visiting a cliff that offers a breathtaking view. The trail guide booklet explores the geology of Algonquin. On the rather steep climb to the top (which means a downhill walk on the return!) one encounters interesting features, including a glacial erratic (a glacier-moved rock) as large as a mobile home! (1.9 km/1.2 miles)

- **Big Pines Trail** KM 40
  As its name suggests, the highlights of this trail are its giant white pines, which at the time of writing are 217 years old. The trail explores the ecology of this species and its importance to Algonquin. The trail also visits the site of a historic logging camp that was active about 120 years ago. (2.9 km/1.9 miles)

Centennial Ridges Trail leads to some of the most impressive vantage points in the Park.

- **Booth's Rock Trail** 9 km (5.6 miles) south from KM 40.3
  Another stunning view is offered from this trail, which also visits two small lakes. After visiting the ruins of the Barclay Estate (complete with tennis courts), the trail returns along the OA&PS Railway bed. The theme of the trail guide is human impact on Algonquin. (5.1 km/3.2 miles)

- **Spruce Bog Boardwalk** KM 42.5
  This short trail is one of the most unusual and one of the easiest to walk. It is now wheel chair-accessible. You can explore the fascinating ecology of a northern bog as you travel through the Sunday Creek bog (on boardwalks). Northern plants, including Labrador tea, and birds such as gray jays highlight this trail. (1.5 km/1 mile)

- **Beaver Pond Trail** KM 45.2
  This trail skirts two beaver ponds and its guide booklet interprets the complex ecology of this Algonquin mammal. This is one of the better wildlife-viewing trails, with hikers occasionally spotting moose and eastern wolves, in addition to beavers, of course! (2.0 km/1.2 miles)

BIKE TRAILS

 The Minnesing Mountain Bike Trail (KM 23) occupies part of the Minnesing Cross Country Ski Trail. Its 23 km (14 miles) of trail traverse a variety of terrain and offer varying degrees of physical challenge.

The Old Railway Bike Trail follows the rail bed of the OA&PS Railway from Mew Lake to Rock Lake. This 10 km (6-mile) hard-surfaced family biking trail can be also reached from the Mew Lake Airfield, the Pog Lake Campground, the Whitefish Mill Site and Rock Lake.

Mountain Bikes can be rented from the Lake of Two Rivers Store (KM 31) and the Opeongo Store (6.2 km/3.9 miles north from KM 46.3).

BACKPACKING TRAILS

 Two excellent backpacking trails can be accessed from the Highway Corridor. While both offer loops that can be walked in one full day (if you are fit and are an accomplished hiker), these trails are primarily for overnight use. Regulations for the Interior apply. Refer to "Other Access Points" (page 196) for details.

Backpacking Trails of Algonquin Provincial Park provides detailed maps and information on these trails. It is available at the Visitor Centre bookstore, at the park gates, or from the Friends of Algonquin (for address see page 215).

- **Western Uplands Backpacking Trail** KM 3
  This is the longest backpacking trail in Algonquin and offers loops ranging from 32 to 88 km (20 to 55 miles). Access to this trail is also achieved from the Rain Lake access, providing backpackers with the option of hiking the trail from Highway 60 to Rain Lake, or vice versa, without returning. As its name suggests, this trail travels through typical West Side hardwood uplands.

- **Highland Backpacking Trail** KM 29.7
  This trail offers loops of 19 and 35 km (12 and 22 miles). The short loop encircles Provoking Lake, while the longer loop also visits Head and Harness lakes.

CROSS COUNTRY SKI TRAILS

In the winter Algonquin is enveloped by a silent beauty not experienced in other seasons. Three fine cross-country trails allow skiers to explore the Park during this invigorating season. All trails have shelters (many with heat available) and emergency barrels (containing first aid kit, spare ski tip, duct tape, matches, fire starter, kindling, candles, emergency blanket, sleeping bag and chocolate bars). Trails are packed and groomed when weather conditions and manpower permit. Levels of challenge are identified on each trail. The free brochure *Algonquin Provincial Park in Winter* details these trails and outlines winter regulations and tips.

■ **Fen Lake Trail (West Gate)**
This trail, which starts at the West Gate, offers loops of 1.25, 5.2 and 13 km (0.8, 3.2 and 8 miles). Much of the trail passes through typical West Side hardwood forest.

■ **Minnesing Trail** KM 23
The return section of the trail follows the historic Minnesing Road, which in early years carried visitors from the Cache Lake railway station to the Minnesing Lodge on Burnt Island Lake. A variety of loops, ranging from 4.7 to 23.4 km (2.9 to 14.5 miles), offer skiers a number of options. The trail traverses diverse terrain and beautiful scenery.

■ **Leaf Lake Trail** KM 53.9
This is a favourite of Algonquin skiers. It passes a large variety of habitats and stunning vistas. By choosing from the selection of loops, one can ski as few as 5 or as many as 17 km (3–10.5 miles) of trail.

■ **Dog Sled Trails** KM 40.3
The Sunday Creek Dog Sled Trail begins in the parking lot of the Big Pines Trail. For details contact the Algonquin Park information office (705-633-5572). See also page 199.

Snowshoes and cross-country skis allow you to experience another dimension of Algonquin's beauty.

PICNIC GROUNDS

 Six picnic grounds are situated along the Corridor. In order of appearance from west to east these are: Oxtongue River (KM 3), Tea Lake Dam (KM 8.1), Canisbay Lake (1 km/0.6 mile north from KM 23.1), Lake of Two Rivers (KM 33.8), East Beach Picnic Area (KM 35.4) and Costello Creek (KM 46.3). While all are kept clean and have outdoor washrooms, some are more aesthetically pleasing because they are situated on water. Perhaps the prettiest of all is the Tea Lake Dam Picnic Ground, situated on the picturesque Oxtongue River. The Lake of Two Rivers sites are also quite nice thanks to their location on a large, scenic lake with good beaches within easy access of the picnic sites. In addition to being found at these official picnic grounds, picnic tables are also available at the Lake of Two Rivers Store (KM 31.4) and at Opeongo Lake (6.2 km/3.9 miles north of KM 46.3).

The East Beach Picnic Area also has a Picnic Pavilion that holds up to a hundred people. It can be rented through the Algonquin Park Information Office (705-633-5562).

RESTAURANTS AND LODGES

 Meals can be purchased along the highway at several locations. Generally, the restaurants do not open until May and are usually open until Thanksgiving, except for the Sunday Creek Café in the Visitor Centre, which is also open throughout the winter. It is best to check in advance of your trip if you will be visiting in the off-season and wish to eat in park facilities. Your needs and your budget will be considerations when choosing a place to eat inside the Park. The three lodges, which serve meals to the general public as well as their guests, tend to offer fine dining and are priced accordingly. You may wish to enquire about prices before committing yourself. (Of course, there are numerous restaurants outside the Park that are open year round.)

All three lodges offer accommodation throughout most of the usual tourist season. Dates of operation and prices can be obtained by phone, by letter or on-line. Addresses are provided in the appendix "Useful Services," page 213.

Here is a list of the facilities that offer meals along or near Highway 60:

- **The Portage Store** KM 14.1
  The restaurant serves light meals, ice cream and alcoholic beverages. The windows overlooking Canoe Lake offer views, sometimes humorous, of canoeists starting or finishing their trips. An adjoining gift shop sells souvenirs. (705-633-5622).

- **Arowhon Pines Lodge** 8 km (5 miles) north from KM 15.4
  The lodge serves full course meals. It is best to reserve (705-633-5661/5662). www.arowhonpines.ca.

- **Bartlett Lodge** south from KM 23.5
  Bartlett Lodge serves full course meals. It is accessible by water only (phone for a boat to pick you up and taxi you to the lodge). Reservations are recommended (705-633-5543). www.bartlettlodge.com.

- **Lake of Two Rivers Store** KM 31.4
  This restaurant specializes in fast food "to go" but it also has a small indoor sit-down section and picnic tables outside (705-633-5373).

- Killarney Lodge KM 33.2
  Full course meals are served here and it is best to phone in advance (705-633-5551). www.killarneylodge.com.

- The Sunday Creek Café KM 43
  Located inside the Algonquin Visitor Centre, this café serves a variety of meals and light snacks, and offers a spectacular view from its dining area.

- The Opeongo Store (Algonquin Outfitters)
  6.2 km (3.6 miles) north from KM 46.3
  The Opeongo sells camping foods, snacks and cold beverages (705-633-5373).

STORES

 Three stores are situated along the Highway Corridor.

- The Portage Store on Canoe Lake KM 14.1
  The Portage Store has a souvenir shop adjoining its restaurant, and a complete outfitting store with canoe and kayak rentals on the lower level. This is one of only two locations in Algonquin where gasoline is available (705-633-5622).

- The Lake of Two Rivers Store KM 31.4
  This store provides a variety of groceries and personal essentials as well as souvenirs. (705-633-5373).

- The Opeongo Store 6.2 km (3.6 miles) north from KM 46.3
  The Opeongo Store is primarily an outfitting store for canoe trippers. It sells a selection of camping foods and cold drinks. Some souvenirs are also available here, as is gasoline for autos and boats. (705-633-5373).

BOOKSTORES

A superb bookstore operated by a co-operating association, the Friends of Algonquin Park, is located at the Algonquin Visitor Centre (KM 43). Publications specifically dealing with Algonquin, most produced by the Friends, are sold here, as well as an excellent selection of natural history, human history and children's books. By becoming a member of the Friends of Algonquin Park you receive a generous 15% off the price of all books in their stores (and you become part of a group that does so very much to help Algonquin Park).

The Friends of Algonquin Park also operates a smaller bookstore at the Algonquin Logging Museum (KM 54.6). Park publications are also available at both East and West gates. In addition, all the stores in the Park offer a small selection of publications.

PUBLIC TELEPHONES

Public pay phones are located at the following places: the East Gate and the West Gate, all campgrounds except Coon Lake, the Algonquin Art Centre (KM 20), the Portage Store (KM 14.1), Cache Lake boat landing (KM 23.5), Lake of Two Rivers Store (KM 31.4), Lake of Two Rivers Picnic Grounds (KM 33.8), the Algonquin Visitor Centre (KM 43), and the Opeongo Store (Algonquin Outfitters) on Opeongo Lake (6.2 km/3.6 miles north from KM 46.3).

CAMPGROUNDS

Nine campgrounds are situated along the Highway 60 in the Corridor. These vary tremendously in size, atmosphere and facilities. Electrical outlets, showers, laundry facilities, flush toilets and a good beach are available at Canisbay (KM 23.1), Mew Lake (KM 30.6), Lake of Two Rivers (KM 31.8), Pog Lake (KM 36.9) and Rock Lake (8 km/5 miles south from KM 40.3) campgrounds. Kearney Lake Campground (KM 36.5) lacks electrical outlets, while Tea Lake Campground (KM 11.4) and Coon Lake Campground (6 km/5.2 miles south from KM 40.3) lack all of the aforementioned facilities. Tea Lake, Lake of Two Rivers and Rock Lake are the only campgrounds where motorboats with up to 20 horsepower motors are allowed on the lake. Lake of Two Rivers and Mew Lake campgrounds are within walking distance of the Lake of Two Rivers Store, which also means that these campgrounds are more exposed to highway noise. The ninth campground, Whitefish Lake Group Campground (accessed from KM 36.9), is available for organized groups on a reservation basis only.

In Canisbay, Mew Lake and Pog Lake campgrounds, certain sites are designated dog-free and radio-free. On sites where dogs are permitted, leashes must be used, as is the regulation all through the Park. Dogs are prohibited on all beaches.

Mew Lake Campground also offers yurts, eight-sided tent structures mounted on insulated wooden deck floors. There are currently seven, each furnished with two sets of bunks that sleep up to six, chairs, table, lights, and an electric heater for fall and winter use. A propane barbecue, dishes, pots, pans, cooking utensils, glasses, tea and coffee pots, and cutlery are provided from May until Canadian Thanksgiving. Yurts can be reserved through Ontario Parks Reservations (1-888-668-7275) or through the Reservation website (www.OntarioParks.com).

If privacy is a priority for you, then I recommend Canisbay as the best and Pog Lake as second-best. Canisbay is situated in a beautiful hardwood forest with relatively isolated sites. Pog Lake Campground lies in a plantation-style pine forest and has many waterfront sites. Both campgrounds have sections that are well distanced from highway noise. Rock Lake and Lake of Two Rivers campgrounds have campsites less isolated from adjoining sites and may be noisier than other campgrounds during the busy period (mid-July to mid-August). Obviously, the type of facilities available and the degree of privacy offered are important factors to consider when choosing a campground.

Firewood is sold at wood yards in Mew and Pog Lake campgrounds, and at the Rock Lake office. During fall and winter, wood is available at Mew Lake.

Canisbay Campground has a feature that is unique. Campsites situated at the north end of the lake can only be reached by canoe. These are known as "paddle-in sites" and offer users a taste of Interior camping.

All campgrounds are open by the middle of June; Tea Lake, Canisbay, Lake of Two Rivers and Rock Lake campgrounds open earlier, and Mew Lake Campground is open year-round.

Each campground has its own pamphlet complete with a map of the sites, and they all have sites that can be reserved. Reservations are recommended for holiday weekends in particular but, while recommended, may not be necessary at other times of the year. Reservations can be made directly at campgrounds or by telephone, year-round, 7 a.m. to 11 p.m. EST, at Ontario Parks Reservations (1-888-688-7275), or on-line: www.OntarioParks.com. A non-refundable reservation fee applies.

MAP 2
HIGHWAY CORRIDOR KM 10–KM 22

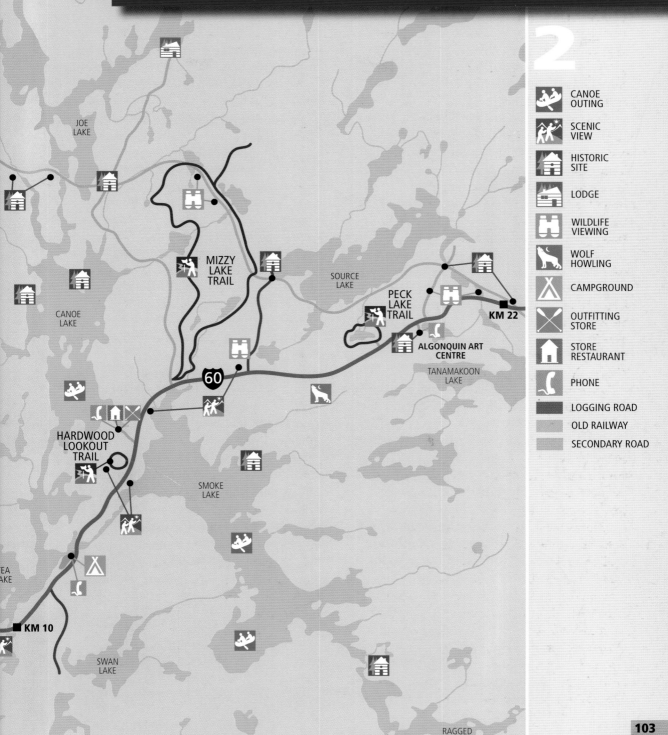

2

- CANOE OUTING
- SCENIC VIEW
- HISTORIC SITE
- LODGE
- WILDLIFE VIEWING
- WOLF HOWLING
- CAMPGROUND
- OUTFITTING STORE
- STORE RESTAURANT
- PHONE
- LOGGING ROAD
- OLD RAILWAY
- SECONDARY ROAD

JOE LAKE

MIZZY LAKE TRAIL

SOURCE LAKE

PECK LAKE TRAIL

KM 22

CANOE LAKE

ALGONQUIN ART CENTRE

TANAMAKOON LAKE

60

HARDWOOD LOOKOUT TRAIL

SMOKE LAKE

TEA LAKE

KM 10

SWAN LAKE

RAGGED LAKE

THE INTERPRETIVE PROGRAM

Algonquin has the reputation of having one of the finest interpretive programs in North America. Conducted walks as well as children's and evening programs are held daily from late June until Labour Day.

Conducted walks are usually a leisurely hour and a half long, and focus on specific subjects such as birds, wildflowers, insects, mushrooms,  trees and forest ecology. In addition, slightly longer outings explore wildlife habitats at special times of day. Evening walks visit excellent habitat for beaver, moose and river otter. Night walks explore the nocturnal activity along a quiet trail, and the wild calls of barred owls are frequently a highlight. Canoe outings are half-day events that explore aquatic habitats. In addition to learning about the natural history of the waterway, participants receive canoe tripping tips.

Algonquin for Kids focuses on the younger audience and deals with topics ranging from reptiles and amphibians to animal defences. These programs are hosted by the Algonquin Visitor Centre. Evening programs are held at the Outdoor Theatre (KM 35.4). They generally last about an hour and a half and consist of two videos and a slide presentation. Topics have included Birds, Loons, Reptiles and Amphibians, Beavers, Eastern Wolves, Moose, Lakes and Fishing, Wildflowers, Tom Thomson and Canoe Tripping. In poor weather the programs are held in the Visitor Centre theatre.

Public Wolf Howls are held on Thursdays in August if wolves and weather permit. On these immensely popular events, participants first attend a talk on wolves and wolf howling at the Outdoor Theatre. They then drive to a site where naturalists attempt to elicit responses from wild wolves by giving vocal imitations of their howls.

Between Labour Day and Thanksgiving interpretive walks and indoor evening programs are offered only on weekends.

All of the locations, times and themes of the events are announced in the weekly flyer *This Week in Algonquin*. This is available in dispensers and posted on bulletin boards throughout the Park, and also appears on the Algonquin Park website (www.algonquinpark.on.ca). A special autumn edition lists all the events for the fall program.

The naturalist staff, seasonal and permanent, are of the highest calibre and are always more than willing to answer any questions concerning Algonquin's flora, fauna or history. If you would like something identified or desire information on any particular aspect of Algonquin, feel free to enquire at the Algonquin Visitor Centre.

Participants in Algonquin's Public Wolf Howls drive to a site where park naturalists "howl up" the wolves.

MAP 3
HIGHWAY CORRIDOR KM 21– KM 38

3

KEARNEY LAKE

KM 38

POG LAKE

OUTDOOR THEATRE

LAKE OF TWO RIVERS

PROVOKING LAKE

TWO RIVERS TRAIL

MEW LAKE

BAT LAKE TRAIL

60

KM 28

JACK LAKE

HEMLOCK BLUFF TRAIL

TRACK & TOWER TRAIL

HIGHLAND BACKPACKING TRAIL

CACHE LAKE

CANISBAY LAKE

POLLY LAKE

MINNESING SKI & MOUNTAIN BIKE TRAIL

SOURCE LAKE

TANAMAKOON LAKE

KM 21

Legend

- HIKING TRAIL
- INTERPRETIVE TRAIL
- CANOE OUTING
- SKI & MOUNTAIN BIKE TRAIL
- SCENIC VIEW
- PICNIC GROUND
- HISTORIC SITE
- LODGE
- WILDLIFE VIEWING
- WOLF HOWLING
- CAMPGROUND
- BIKE TRAIL
- STORE RESTAURANT
- PHONE
- LOGGING ROAD
- OLD RAILWAY
- SECONDARY ROAD

105

WILDLIFE-VIEWING AREAS

Many of Algonquin's interpretive trails and outings offer excellent opportunities to catch a glimpse of some of its famed wildlife. Perhaps the two finest trails for general wildlife viewing are Beaver Pond and Mizzy Lake, both situated along Highway 60. Each offers a mixture of habitats, including ponds supporting active beaver colonies and superb summer moose-feeding sites. Wolves also frequent these areas in some years, particularly in late summer. In fact, Wolf Howl Pond on the Mizzy Lake Trail is so named because eastern wolves are commonly heard howling from the boggy meadows at the northwest end of the pond. River otters are also often seen, particularly in the waterways along the Mizzy Lake Trail.

If encountering wildlife is one of the goals of your trip, refer to "Observing Wildlife" (page 47) for tips and advice on general wildlife viewing. Many of the species can be attracted with specific calls and noises, and these are outlined in this chapter. "Wildlife-viewing Etiquette" (page 50) offers suggestions on how to avoid disturbing the animals while you are observing them.

The following is a discussion of sites for some of the more popular species. For simplicity, these suggested sites are listed starting from the west end of Highway 60.

Moose

The Highway 60 Corridor can be as good as – at times perhaps even better than – the Interior for seeing moose, the great monarchs of the north. Many of these giants discover that the roadside ditches are enriched with sodium in the form of salt from winter road maintenance, and thus can be readily found from April through June along the highway, gleaning this essential nutrient from the water in muddy ditches.

From June through to late July, moose can often be spotted, particularly in the evening or at dawn, in a number of lakes, ponds and streams along the highway when they seek out their natural source of sodium in the leaves of water plants, especially those of water-shield. I recommend checking Eucalia Lake (KM 39) and the pond opposite the turn-off for the Opeongo Road (KM 46.3). In addition, the Opeongo Road, north of the bridge where Costello Creek flows under the road (approximately 3 km/2 miles north of the highway), frequently offers views of moose feeding in their favourite settings.

Perhaps the two best trails for viewing moose in the summer are the Mizzy Lake Trail (KM 15.4), particularly along the abandoned OA&PS Railway bed that forms the northeastern section of the trail, and the Beaver Pond Trail (KM 45.2).

Although they may be seen anywhere along the roadside, more of these magnificent animals appear east of the Algonquin Art Centre (KM 20) than west of it. In addition to the sites discussed above, some areas along the Highway Corridor where frequent sightings have been made, particularly in early summer, include:

- **Cache Lake region** KM 22.3–KM 23.8

- **Track and Tower Trail region** KM 25

- **Hemlock Bluff Trail region** KM 27.2–KM 27.6

- **Kearney Campground to Eucalia Lake** KM 36.5–KM 39

- **Eos Lake to Beaver Pond Trail** KM 43.8–KM 45.2

- **West Smith Lake to the Algonquin Logging Museum** KM 51.5–KM 54.6

Moose are most easily observed in late spring when they seek salt in roadside ditches.

Eastern Wolf

Although among the most difficult to see of all of Algonquin's large animals, eastern wolves are, at certain times of the year, among the easiest to locate by their vocalizations.

From late July until mid-October, wolves are often heard right from Highway 60, as many nearby beaver meadows and boggy sites are used as rendezvous sites (see "The Nature of Wolves," page 60). At these locations, the pups are very vocal and readily respond to human howls (see "When and How to See Wildlife," page 52, for a discussion on howling).

Try listening or howling from the following locations:

■ **Western Uplands Backpacking Trail** KM 3
Try from the bridge across the Oxtongue River at the start of the trail.

■ **Highway 60** at KM 8
Try just past the bridge on the gated road that leads north.

■ **Arowhon Road,** 4.5 km (2.7 miles) north from KM 15.4.
Try at the intersection of this road and the Old Railway.

■ **Highway 60** at KM 18
The bogs stretching to the south from this point occasionally have wolves.

■ **Rock Lake Road** at KM 40.3
Try at the intersection of the highway and the Rock Lake Road; also try 2.8 km (1.7 miles) south on the Rock Lake Road.

- **Sunday Creek** KM 42.6
  The top of the rock cut just west of Sunday Creek and on the north side of the highway is an outstanding site. The eastern edge of the rock has a gradual slope easily climbed – but do be careful and use a flashlight at night.

- **Eos Lake** KM 43.8
  Wolves are regularly heard to the north of the lake.

- **Beaver Pond Trail** KM 45.2
  Wolves have been heard from either side of the highway near the trail entrance.

- **Opeongo Road** KM 46.3
  Try at the junction of the highway and the Opeongo Road; also try approximately 3 km (2 miles) north from the highway where the Opeongo Road crosses Costello Creek.

- **Brewer Lake** KM 48.6
  I have only heard wolves here a couple of times but the incredible echoes from across the lake make this an enjoyable spot to try. This location is special to me, as it is where I saw my very first wolf. I was in good company that night – I was howling with Russ Rutter (co-author of *World of the Wolf*), Ron Tozer (renowned former park naturalist), and Pat Tozer (former manager of the Friends of Algonquin Park).

- **Highway 60** at KM 54
  Wolves are regularly heard from this location, usually to the north of the road.

- **Highway 60** at KM 56.9
  Wolves are regularly heard howling from the small lake at the end of the short road that leads west.

Although the above locations might offer the best chances of finding wolves, these elusive animals have been heard at many other sites along the Corridor, including right from several of the highway campgrounds. However, I would not recommend howling within earshot of these busy spots, particularly at one a.m!

Because you will be stopping along the highway, you must be safety-conscious. Beware of soft shoulders on the roadside, but never stop on the pavement. If possible, pull off in parking lots of trails or picnic sites. Stand well away from the highway when you are enjoying this magnificent music of the wilds.

Public Wolf Howls, excursions to hear wolves in the Corridor, are held on Thursdays in August if wolves have been located and weather permits. As a Wolf Howl is not attempted unless the naturalist staff has confirmed the presence of wolves on the previous night, it is not disclosed until each Thursday morning whether there will be a howl. To determine if a howl is being held on that day, either enquire at the Visitor Centre or any other park facility, or check the weekly bulletin *This Week in Algonquin* (issued each Thursday morning). If a Wolf Howl is not held, an evening program on wolves will be offered instead. To avoid interfering with the Public Howls, I recommend that in August you do not go howling on Tuesdays, Wednesdays or Thursdays in the Highway 60 Corridor. On those days you might try another part of Algonquin, such as the Basin Depot area.

Red Fox

People regularly encounter relatively tame red foxes in Algonquin. Their tameness is invariably due to frequent contact with humans and not to disease. Regardless, one should always be cautious and not touch or feed one of these animals. Although foxes are most active after sunset, they

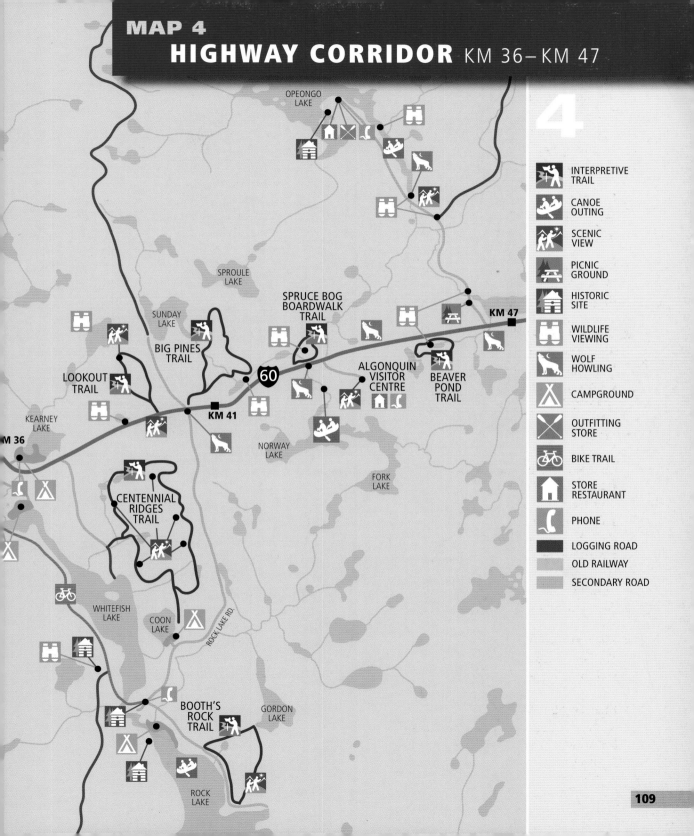

MAP 4
HIGHWAY CORRIDOR KM 36– KM 47

4

OPEONGO LAKE

SPROULE LAKE

SPRUCE BOG BOARDWALK TRAIL

SUNDAY LAKE

BIG PINES TRAIL

KM 47

LOOKOUT TRAIL

60

KM 41

ALGONQUIN VISITOR CENTRE

BEAVER POND TRAIL

KEARNEY LAKE

KM 36

NORWAY LAKE

FORK LAKE

CENTENNIAL RIDGES TRAIL

WHITEFISH LAKE

COON LAKE

ROCK LAKE RD.

BOOTH'S ROCK TRAIL

GORDON LAKE

ROCK LAKE

Symbol	Description
	INTERPRETIVE TRAIL
	CANOE OUTING
	SCENIC VIEW
	PICNIC GROUND
	HISTORIC SITE
	WILDLIFE VIEWING
	WOLF HOWLING
	CAMPGROUND
	OUTFITTING STORE
	BIKE TRAIL
	STORE RESTAURANT
	PHONE
	LOGGING ROAD
	OLD RAILWAY
	SECONDARY ROAD

109

may be encountered in early morning or late evening. Probably the best way to find them is to slowly drive the highway after sunset and watch for their greenish eye-shine glowing along the edges of the road.

One pair of red foxes often dens on or near the airfield at Mew Lake (KM 30.6). Thus, they are often seen in the Lake of Two Rivers and Mew Lake section of Highway 60. Another pair regularly dens near the East Gate (KM 56), so it is common to see foxes there. Another good area for seeing red foxes is along the highway near the Rock Lake turn (KM 40.3).

Black Bear

Although relatively common all through the Park, black bears are usually quite difficult to spot primarily because of their shyness. Fortunate visitors might view a bear in early morning or late evening, the optimum times for encountering one crossing the road or foraging along open edges.

The best time of the year for seeing black bears in Algonquin is from mid-July to mid-August, when the raspberries, blueberries and cherries ripen. During this period, it is worth taking a slow drive along the Opeongo and Rock Lake roads. In some years bears can be observed from campsite 112 in Kearney Lake Campground, eating berries on the open hillside across the creek.

Very infrequently, bears are encountered feeding in berry patches along the interpretive trails, particularly Centennial Ridges. They are usually long gone before you are even aware that they were present. By walking the trails as silently as possible (for if the bears hear you coming they quickly vanish) either very early or late in the day, you will increase your slight chances of seeing a black bear.

One area to check during the berry season is the old mill site at Whitefish Lake. This site is accessed by travelling south on the Rock Lake Road until you reach the campground office. Park here and walk along the gated road on your right, which is part of the Old Railway Bike Trail. You will come to a bridge crossing the Madawaska River. Cross the bridge and continue along the left branch of the road to the large open area where a sawmill once stood. This has been a popular foraging location for bears.

Beaver

Algonquin is home to thousands of beaver colonies. The beaver is such a common and important animal in Algonquin that one of the Park's interpretive trails, the Beaver Pond Trail, is dedicated to its natural history. This trail is not only an excellent spot to see beavers in the early evening (when they begin their nightly activity) but it is also an excellent place to learn about them, for their fascinating ecology is detailed in the trail guide booklet.

Many of the lakes and ponds along Highway 60 also harbour beavers. They can commonly be observed right through the car window – a particularly enjoyable method during the biting fly season.

Don't be surprised if some of the highway beavers sport "earrings" in the form of silver tags in their ears. Ear-tagged beavers along the Corridor were part of former university research programs.

Some of the traditional spots (in addition to the Beaver Pond Trail) in the Corridor are:

- **Pond** 1km (0.6 mile) north from KM 8. Walk along the road, closed to private vehicles, until you reach the pond on your left. Be aware that in recent years this area has been used for discarding road-killed moose.

- **Mew Lake** KM 30.1

- **Eucalia Lake** KM 39

  If visiting this excellent pond for beavers, be sure to park on the wider road shoulders below or above – not alongside – the guard rails bordering the pond.

- **Rock Lake Road** KM 40.3

  At time of writing, beavers inhabit the creek on the east side of the road where it meets Highway 60. It is worth checking the creek farther south on the Rock Lake Road as well.

- **Ring-neck Pond** KM 41.2

  You may not see the lodge hidden along the far shore at the west end of the pond but you will easily see the one near the tall pine at the east end.

- **Opeongo Road** north from KM 46.3

  The best sites to check are the sections of Hermit Creek, which follows the left (west) side of the Opeongo Road as you travel north, the section of Costello Creek just past the bridge that crosses it approximately 3 km (2 miles) north of the highway, and the area where Costello Creek enters Opeongo Lake. The latter spot can be viewed either from the boat launches to the south of the Opeongo Store or from the road just before it enters the store and boat launch access area.

- **West Smith Pond** KM 53

  You will see the dam and the lodge to the north of the highway. An unmarked road just west of this location leads in to the west end of the pond.

River Otter

It can be a challenge to find river otters in Algonquin, despite their frequent appearance in waterways along the Corridor. They are more easily viewed in late summer and fall when family groups are travelling together, or in early spring when individuals are feeding along the edges of the receding ice. Otters range widely, so it is difficult to predict where they will be from day to day. However, in early spring (mid-April to mid-May) they are commonly seen along the edge of the ice when the lakes begin to open, and may frequent good feeding areas for several days or more. At that time of year it is useful to check any waterway for dark debris on the edge of the ice. These dark piles may be droppings or remains of meals indicating the presence of otters.

Otters can be encountered anywhere open water is visible. Hermit and Costello creeks along the Opeongo Road (north from KM 46.3) are among the most reliable spots for seeing them. The best area is along Costello Creek between the bridge that crosses the creek approximately 3 km (2 miles) north of the highway and the south end of Opeongo Lake. They are also occasionally observed on the logs in Costello Lake across from the Costello Picnic Ground. Other areas where you might see river otters are:

- **The Mizzy Lake Trail** KM 15.4

  Mizzy is without question the best trail for encountering otters. They might be seen in any of the nine ponds visible from the trail. In particular, Mizzy Lake and Wolf Howl Pond offer excellent viewing opportunities.

- **Pond** at KM 21.4

  The pond on the north side of the highway occasionally has otters.

- **Mew Lake** KM 30.1

- **Lake of Two Rivers Campground** KM 31.8

  Otters are frequently present where the Madawaska River enters the lake.

- **Ringneck Pond** KM 41.2

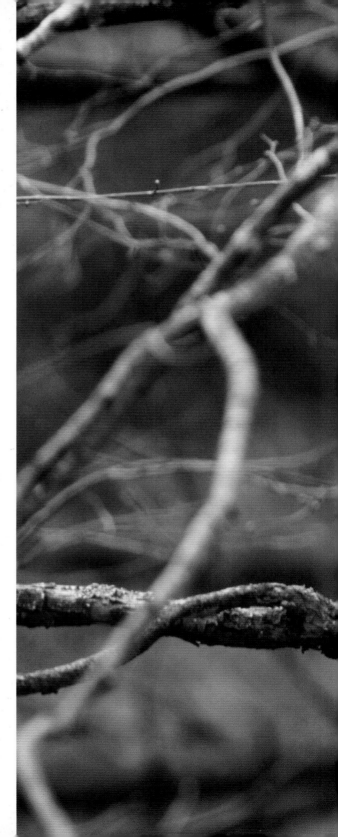

ALGONQUIN BIRDS

With its diverse array of habitats, particularly the mixture of northern coniferous and southern deciduous forests, Algonquin boasts an amazing mixture of species. More than half of the 276 species recorded within the Park have been known to breed here. The majority of the nesting species can usually be encountered by searching in the proper habitat, although frequently they are more easily heard than seen.

Two of the park publications, *Birds of Algonquin Provincial Park* and *The Checklist and Seasonal Status of the Birds of Algonquin Provincial Park*, are invaluable for enjoying birds in Algonquin. The first discusses birds by habitat and includes excellent colour photographs of 77 of the more common species. The latter summarizes all the species recorded up to its most recent printing and provides useful bar graphs detailing their dates of occurrence.

Because of the popularity of Algonquin's birds, the interpretive program offers early morning interpretive bird walks and an evening program titled "The Birds of Algonquin." Most of the interpretive trails traverse a variety of habitats and thus offer a variety of birds. My favourite trails for birdwatching are the Whiskey Rapids and Beaver Pond trails. Spruce Bog Boardwalk and Mizzy Lake are two of the best trails for encountering northern species. Valuable tips on finding birds can be found in "Observing Wildlife" (page 47).

Most birders come to Algonquin to see the northern specialties (birds whose range does not extend much farther south than Algonquin). With this in mind, I mention some of the better locations along the Corridor for a few of these species. In addition, I suggest sites for encountering other popular species.

Barred owls, the most common owls in Algonquin, are the only ones to have completely dark eyes.

Spruce Grouse

This tame northern grouse prefers the cool dark recesses of northern bogs and black spruce forests (although jack pine forests on the East Side are excellent sites also). For many birders, Algonquin is the place of their first (and frequently only) sighting of this northern grouse.

The males are at their ornate finest during the breeding season in April and early May. They strut around with their red eye combs inflamed and their tails fanning noisily open and closed. Males also perform loud "flutter flights" from the ground up to a nearby conifer and back down again. This unmistakable sound makes it relatively easy to find a displaying bird. Some males begin to display again in early fall, but it is a more subdued performance. Recordings of female calls will attract the males, especially in the spring. But before trying this, read the third item in "Wildlife-viewing Etiquette" (page 50).

Spruce Grouse are frequently observed eating the needles of spruces and other conifers. Early morning and late afternoon are times of increased feeding activity in summer. From mid August to mid-September they commonly feed on tamarack needles. In late fall and winter they prefer the needles of spruce and pine. When searching for these birds, scan from the ground level to about 7 metres (25 feet) high on the branches of coniferous trees and listen for the snapping of needles while they are feeding. When flushed, they exhibit a noisy, heavy flight that is generally short in duration. An excellent article on finding this species, by Ron Tozer and Ron Pittaway, appears in *Ontario Birds,* Vol. 8, Number 2, copies of which are available upon request at the Visitor Centre.

There are several excellent places for searching for these often-elusive birds. I list them according to general ease in finding the birds (do keep in mind, however, that in any of these sites the grouse might be either surprisingly easy or impossibly difficult to locate).

- **Spruce Bog Boardwalk Trail** KM 42.5
  This has traditionally been one of the best spots along the highway for spruce grouse. While you may encounter the birds along any part of the trail, there are at least two sections where observations have been made more frequently. Between Post #1 and the open bog mat before Post #2, there is an island of drier, more open ground with a number of footpaths, particularly on the left (north) side, created by grouse seekers. Another good section lies between Post #6 and Post #7, especially near the trail register box.

- **Mizzy Lake Trail** KM 15.4
  An excellent area for viewing Spruce Grouse lies along the northern section of the trail in the Wolf Howl Pond vicinity. You can get to this area by walking the trail (highly recommended for its diversity of birds), or by driving north 4.5 km (2.8 miles) on the Arowhon Road to the Old Railway bed junction and turning right. When you reach a locked gate, be sure to park to the side, not blocking the road. Proceed east on foot for approximately 1 km (0.6 mile) to Wolf Howl Pond. Spruce grouse can frequently be seen either right on the rail bed picking up grit, or feeding in the conifers fringing the rail bed. The section of rail bed just west of Wolf Howl Pond is good, but the 100 metres (110 yards) or so of rail bed southeast of Post #6 may produce the best results, either along or just off of the rail bed, which is part of the Mizzy Lake Trail.

The inflated red skin comb over the eye of this spruce grouse indicates that it is in breeding mode.

■ Opeongo Road KM 46.3

There are two excellent locations along this road for spotting spruce grouse, which are often seen picking up grit along the edge of the road, particularly at daybreak. However, a search through the spruces just off the road may sometimes be required. The first place to check is the spruce woods bordering the left (west) side of the road 2.5 km (1.5 miles) north of the highway. Grouse may be found from this point for about another 0.5 km (0.3 mile) north, although the stretch from here to the orange gate on the road usually offers the best opportunities.

The second area worth checking is along the right (east) side of the road approximately 0.5 km (0.3 mile) north of where Costello Creek crosses under the road. The birds usually reside in the strip of spruces between the road and the open bog mat to the east.

■ Davies' Bog KM 30

If you still haven't succeeded, another area to check is the coniferous forest surrounding Davies' Bog. This is usually a difficult spot to find them in but they are here! The best way to get to this area is to walk the Bat Lake Trail in reverse to Post #12. You might see spruce grouse on the trail but odds are some searching will be required. Try scouring the spruces on either end of the boardwalk at Post #12.

Gray Jay

This northern bird is a delight to encounter not only because of its gentle nature but also because it will unabashedly take food from your hand. At times it seems hard to believe that a bird so seemingly meek of disposition could survive through the severe Algonquin winters. Yet gray jays do so quite nicely, principally because they ceaselessly store food through the other seasons. It is fascinating to watch the birds in action. After accepting a morsel of bread, cookie, raisin – or whatever your offering might be – the jay rolls each piece in its mouth, coating it with saliva. It then flies off to stash the package in a tree, frequently under a piece of lichen or loose bark. The saliva cements the package securely in its hiding place (which is occasionally robbed by blue jays, experts in shadowing their cousins). This sticky coating may also serve to keep the food fresh, for it could be many months before the stash is eaten.

When gray jays approach you for handouts, you may notice that their legs are decorated with colourful bands that jingle-jangle when they fly. Dan Strickland, former long-time Chief Park Naturalist, has been studying these birds for about 40 years. By banding the young each spring, he has been able to document not only how long they live, but also where they range, and even such personal information as whom they mate with!

This amazing study is one of the longest of its kind and is truly a labour of love for Strickland. You can help out by recording the date of your sighting, its location and the coloured band combinations on each of their legs. Each colour provides a letter, with the left leg's combination given first. For example, one of Strickland's birds is ROSLYOGR; the letters indicate that it wears a red band over a standard aluminum band on its left leg (a standard aluminum band is always present on one of the legs) and a yellow band over a dark green one on its right leg. Thus, GOSLBOOR wears green over standard on the left leg, blue over orange on the right. Your valuable observations can be dropped off at the Visitor Centre or at either gate, whichever is most convenient for you.

Since gray jays frequent much the same habitat as spruce grouse, it comes as no surprise that you may well encounter both species in the same area. Thus, any of the aforementioned areas for seeing grouse might produce jays. Unfortunately, there are times, particularly in late spring and early summer, when gray jays become secretive and tough to find, even in the best of locations. They become easier to find as summer progresses and you are virtually guaranteed to encounter them in fall and winter. Refer to "Observing Wildlife" (page 47) for tips on how you might attract them (although these birds tend to find you first!) and be sure to carry some spare food with you. Some regular "hot spots" to try are:

- **Opeongo Road** KM 46.3
  Several pairs of gray jays have territories along this road. While you may encounter them almost anywhere on this road, try the Costello Picnic Grounds, at the junction of the logging road 2.5 km (1.5 miles) north of the highway, and just past the bridge where Costello Creek passes under the road, 3 km (2 miles) north of the highway.

- **Mizzy Lake Trail** KM 15.4
  The Old Railway at the northeastern section of the trail is the best area for jays. They can usually be found between Wolf Howl Pond and West Rose Lake.

- **Spruce Bog Boardwalk Trail** KM 42.5
  The birds might find you virtually anywhere along this trail.

- **Mew Lake Campground** KM 30.6
  Try walking through the campground, particularly in fall and winter, when campers maintain bird feeders.

Gray jays, Algonquin's friendliest birds, usually find you before you find them.

Black-backed Woodpecker

Another "northerner" frequently sought out by birders is the black-backed woodpecker. It also inhabits the coniferous habitat of the former two species.

These birds are most easily encountered by listening for their heavy slow pecking and their sharp calls (resembling a short, noisy kiss to the back of your fingers). The best way, though, is to imitate or play back the call of a barred owl. Not only does this call draw in black-backs but it also is guaranteed to attract any other woodpecker within hearing range. (Before using playbacks read "Wildlife-viewing Etiquette," page 50.)

An aid to finding these birds involves the distinctive signs they leave behind when feeding. Among their favoured foods are the larvae of bark beetles, which, as their name suggests, tunnel under the bark of trees. Black-backed woodpeckers particularly relish the species that inhabits spruce trees. To get at the beetles, these woodpeckers strip the bark from infected trees. Thus, if you find spruce trees with large sections of the trunk recently stripped clean (the barkless trunk appearing orange), the woodpecker is probably not far away. These birds are year-round residents and in summer they frequently nest in the vicinity of beaver ponds.

Sites where you might encounter black-backed woodpeckers include all of the places described for spruce grouse, especially the northeastern section of the Mizzy Lake Trail and along the Opeongo Road. I would also recommend that you search at these other locations.

■ **Western Uplands Backpacking Trail** KM 3
  The section of the trail just past the bridge at the trail head is an excellent place for these birds.

■ **Oxtongue Logging Road Pond** KM 8
  This road, closed to private vehicles, leads north from the highway. Park either on the shoulder of the highway or to the side of the gate, leaving the access unobstructed. Walk approximately 1 km (0.6 mile) along the road until you arrive at a large pond on the left. Black-backed woodpeckers are frequently encountered in the vicinity of the pond. (Be aware that in recent years this area has been used for discarding road-killed moose.)

Boreal Chickadee

These northern counterparts of black-capped chickadees become extremely silent and thus very difficult to find during the nesting season. However, as summer progresses they become increasingly vocal, and by mid-August their wheezy calls allow them to be found in most of the locations frequented by spruce grouse and black-backed woodpeckers.

In addition to the locations listed for those species try also the following sites:

■ **Mew Lake Airfield** KM 30.6
  Look around the south edge.

■ **Road leading north** from KM 30.6
  (you can only walk on this restricted road).

■ **The Old Railway** on the north side of the Highway at KM 22.3.

■ **The Algonquin Logging Museum** KM 54.6
  Look along the trail that goes around the museum.

OTHER BIRDS

A few more commonly sought-after species are profiled here. Additional information about any of the park birds can be obtained from the naturalists at the Visitor Centre.

Barred Owl

The booming calls and eerie cackles of the barred owl, Algonquin's most common owl, are regularly heard at night. This species readily responds to human imitations and to playbacks of recorded calls (like those found on the inexpensive CD *Voices of Algonquin*). Before using playbacks, refer to "Wildlife-viewing Etiquette" (page 50). Barred owls are also easily attracted by "squeaking" particularly just before sunset. (Refer to "When and How to See Wildlife," page 52.)

You may wish to participate in an interpretive night walk if one is offered during your stay, for barred owls frequently make their presence known on these outings.

While you might hear these birds virtually anywhere in the Highway Corridor, here is a list of some of the better locations:

- **Western Uplands Backpacking Trail** KM 3
  Try from the bridge at the beginning of the trail.

- **Whiskey Rapids Trail** KM 7.2
  I have often heard Barred Owls from the highway near the trail entrance.

- **Hardwood Hill** KM 16.7
  Traditional areas to hear these birds are along the highway and on the logging road that leads north.

- **Source Lake Road** KM 20.1
  Approximately 0.4 km (0.2 mile) north of the Highway is a good place to try.

- **Hemlock Bluff Trail** KM 27.2
  Barred owls have been heard from both sides of the highway at this location.

- **Trailer Sanitation Station** KM 35.6
  Try near the open area approximately 0.5 km (0.3 mile) north of the Sanitation turnaround.

- **Rock Lake Road** KM 40.3
  Try at the intersection of this road and Highway 60. Also try 1 km (0.6 mile) up the road on the north side of the highway, at the gate marking the end to public travel on this road.

- **Spruce Bog Boardwalk Trail** KM 42.5
  I enjoy listening from the top of the rock cut that lies between the parking lot and the bridge crossing the creek. The eastern edge of the rocks has a gradual slope but do be careful in climbing up and be sure to use a flashlight at night. This is also a great spot for hearing wolves and watching fireflies and shooting stars.

- **Brewer Lake** KM 48.6
  The parking lot offers safe parking as well as an excellent listening location.

- **Leaf Lake Ski Trail** KM 53.9
  I have often heard barred owls in the vicinity of the trail entrance.

Merlin

Once rare in the Park, the numbers of these agile falcons have increased dramatically and they can be found nesting in pines near most major lakes. Listen for their rapidly repeated high-pitched screams and watch for their large-headed silhouette atop dead tree snags. In recent years particularly good sites have been:

- **Lake of Two Rivers Picnic Site** KM 33.8
- **Rock Lake,** 8 km (5 miles) south from KM 40.3
- **Algonquin Visitor Centre Road** KM 43
- **Opeongo Lake,** north from KM 46.3

Pileated Woodpecker

These spectacular crow-sized woodpeckers are common throughout Algonquin and are frequently encountered along Highway 60. Their distinctive feeding excavations, large (often gigantic!) rectangular or oval holes made in search of carpenter ants, are easily found in a number of dead trees right along the highway. Listen for their distinctive *kuk-kuk-kuk* calls. An imitation of these calls or a barred owl call may attract the birds.

Pileated woodpeckers frequently fly across the highway in late afternoon. Their stiff flight with massive wings flashing bold black and white patterns is quite distinctive.

These birds can be spotted along any trail, particularly (but not exclusively) on trails through mature hardwood forests. Some locations where pileated woodpeckers are commonly seen include:

- **Hardwood Lookout Trail** KM 13.8
- **Found Lake** KM 20
  A trail that starts directly behind the buildings of the Algonquin Art Centre and circles Found Lake.

- **Highway 60** between KM 25.5 and KM 26.3
- **Highway 60** between KM 28.5 and KM 28.8
- **Rock Lake Road,** south from KM 40.3
- **Booth's Rock Trail,** 9 km (5.5 miles) south from KM 40.3

Common Loon

Rare is the Algonquin campsite from which the mournful wails and haunting laughter of a loon cannot be heard at night. This is a relatively easy bird to encounter because virtually all lakes – even the busiest ones – support at least one pair. The CD *Voices of Algonquin* not only has outstanding recordings of these birds but also offers explanations as to what the different calls mean.

Because common loons nest at the edge of the water, canoeists not infrequently discover their nests. If you do come across a nest, do not spend more than a brief moment admiring the birds before you leave them in privacy. Repeated harassment, regardless of how unintentional it might be, may result in a loss of the eggs. Park naturalists keep annual records of loon sightings, so be sure to report your observations to the Visitor Centre staff. "The Nature of Loons" (page 72) provides more information on this species.

Loons can be found on most park lakes. Traditional viewing sites include:

- **Smoke Lake** KM 15.2
- **Lake of Two Rivers** KM 32.3 to KM 33; KM 33.8; KM 34.5
- **Costello Lake** KM 46.3
- **Brewer Lake** KM 48.6

MAP 5
HIGHWAY CORRIDOR South from KM 40.3

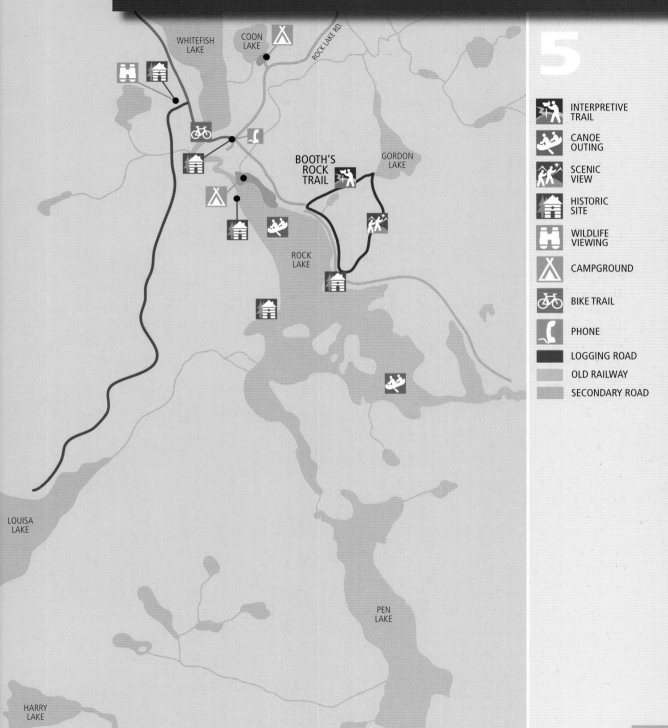

WHITEFISH LAKE

COON LAKE

ROCK LAKE RD.

BOOTH'S ROCK TRAIL

GORDON LAKE

ROCK LAKE

LOUISA LAKE

PEN LAKE

HARRY LAKE

5

INTERPRETIVE TRAIL

CANOE OUTING

SCENIC VIEW

HISTORIC SITE

WILDLIFE VIEWING

CAMPGROUND

BIKE TRAIL

PHONE

LOGGING ROAD

OLD RAILWAY

SECONDARY ROAD

SCENIC VIEWS

The Highway 60 Corridor is rich in striking scenery and breathtaking vantage points at all times of the year, with each season dressing the landscape in the latest colours. In late summer, roadside lakes come alive with swirling mists. In autumn, maple hills transform into an extravaganza of fiery colour. In winter, fresh snows smother the trees with a blanket of white. The following is a guide to some of the more dramatic locations for viewing or photographing scenery along the Highway Corridor. Of course, beauty lies in the eye of the beholder, and you undoubtedly will find a number of additional and near the highway the highway that particularly appeal to you.

- **Tea Lake** KM 9.2
  The only drawback to this site is the telephone lines along the lake side of the highway.

- **Smoke Creek** KM 12.0
  This creek offers excellent fall colours along its edge and also watery reflections of them, particularly early in the morning. The old parking lot on the east side of the bridge is the best spot for enjoying this view.

- **Smoke Lake** KM 13.5
  A good view of maple hills and Smoke Lake is obtained from this point on the highway.

- **Hardwood Lookout Trail** KM 13.8
  As its name suggests, this trail has a lookout over hardwood hills and Smoke Lake. While the view from this trail is satisfying, those afforded by other trails that offer lookouts are generally more dynamic.

Rock, water and August mist combine to make this point on Smoke Lake a classic Algonquin scene.

- **Smoke Lake** KM 14.8

  The pull-off on the lake side is an ideal place to park. At daybreak in August, the sun rises just behind the point jutting into Smoke Lake. The mists that rise off the lake at this time of year create an unforgettable backdrop.

- **Hardwood Hill** KM 16.6

  The view looking west is particularly stunning during the peak of the fall colours.

- **Track and Tower Trail** KM 25

  A superb view of Cache Lake can be enjoyed at Post #7.

- **Two Rivers Hill** KM 28.5

  This view to the east is particularly attractive at daybreak. Mists frequently shroud the far hills, and the pine at the lower left of the hill projects nicely against this backdrop. The beautiful hardwood forest covering the hillside along the north side of the road is especially photogenic in the autumn.

- **Two Rivers Trail** KM 31

  You will reach a fine lookout point at Post #7.

- **Lake of Two Rivers** KM 32.5

  Various points along the road offer excellent views of the lake. The far side of the lake is alive with colour in the fall. This is also a spectacular spot at daybreak, particularly during the mists of late summer.

- **Centennial Ridges Trail** 2 km (1.2 miles) south from KM 37.6

  Some of the finest vantage points in the Corridor are situated along this rugged trail.

- **Lookout Trail** KM 39.7

  An excellent view of the rolling hills typical of this side of the Park is available from the highway itself. Even after the maples have faded, this site still offers colourful views, for the hills then blaze with golden poplars. At the top of this walking trail, you will find one of the most dramatic views of the western uplands. In addition, an unmarked trail leading to a fine view starts out directly across the highway from the west end of the parking lot. All lookouts lack railings, so do keep children under control at all times.

- **Booth's Rock Trail** 9 km (5.5 miles) south of KM 40.3.

  The view over Rock Lake from Post #7 is stunning.

- **Algonquin Visitor Centre** KM 45

  The viewing deck at the Visitor Centre offers a breathtaking panorama, equally splendid at any time of the year.

- **Costello Creek** 3.5 km (2.1 miles) north from KM 46.3.

  This boggy creek with a dramatic cliff rising behind it is a beautiful area year round. Several sites along the road offer enjoyable views, especially in late summer and fall. My favourite spot is just beyond the bridge where the creek passes under the road.

- **Brewer Lake** KM 48.6

  The hillside across the lake displays some of the best fall colour along the Highway. If you climb to the top of the rock cut on the north side of the highway, you will discover an even more spectacular view.

- **West Smith Pond** KM 53

  On the north side of the road lies a lovely beaver pond with dam and lodge in view. Early morning mists often rise from the water, creating a living canvas that is reminiscent of a Group of Seven painting.

POINTS OF HISTORICAL INTEREST

 Algonquin has had a long and fascinating history, and artifacts from the past are often found right along the highway.

The following is a brief guide to some of the more interesting historic sites located in the Corridor. Other sites in the highway vicinity but accessible only by canoe will be discussed under Canoeing in the Corridor.

The Ottawa, Arnprior & Parry Sound Railway (OA&PS)

The rail bed of this historic railway, reputed to have been one of the busiest in Canada with a train every 20 minutes, can be viewed at several locations. Sections of the rail bed are now parts of three interpretive trails, two backpacking trails and a bike trail.

J.R. Booth, a lumber entrepreneur prominent in the Park's history, built the railway between 1894 and 1896. It was initially used for hauling

The historic Ottawa, Arnprior & Parry Sound Railway forms the northern leg of the Mizzy Lake Trail.

logs and grain, but it soon became important for transporting visitors to Algonquin. It remained the only way to access the Park until the arrival of Highway 60 in the mid-1930s.

The easy access provided by the new highway became the nemesis of the OA&PS. Train service between Lake of Two Rivers and Cache Lake was discontinued in 1933. Service from the east to Lake of Two Rivers was terminated in 1946, and from the west to Cache Lake in 1959.

For simplicity, I mention access points to the old rail bed starting from the west end of the Park.

Mizzy Lake Trail KM 15.4
The northeast section of the trail lies on the rail bed. This can also be accessed by driving up the Arowhon Road approximately 4.5 km (2.7 miles) to a crossroads. The road crossing the Arowhon Road is the rail bed of the OA&PS Railway.

Source Lake Road KM 20.1
Drive north until you come to the dip at the Madawaska River (here just a small creek) crossing. The railway abutments are clearly visible on either side of the road.

Highway 60 Crossing KM 22.3
You will find a small parking area on the north side of the road (you may see cars parked in a private lot on the south side of the road, but this is for the staff of a girls' camp, Camp Tanamakoon). Although the railway actually crosses the highway, only the section on the north side is walkable. Look for a footpath leading off to the northwest (as you face the woods it will be to your left). After travelling through an alder thicket you will enter an open area where the rail bed becomes very apparent. If you continue, you will eventually reach the Source Lake Road.

Cache Lake KM 23

Drive into the Cache Lake parking lot. When you approach the boat launch, you can easily see the rail bed to your left (behind the shelter). To the right lies the former Highland Inn, a once grand railway hotel. A planned Cache Lake Historic Site will feature a reconstructed rail track and five display panels depicting the site's history. The hotel was built in 1908 and expanded in 1910. This elegant building was demolished in 1957, around the same time that the rail service from the west was discontinued. All that remain are a few walls bordering the railway platform, moss-covered stairs leading up to the site of the inn and an old fire hydrant. If you travel east along the rail bed, you will eventually arrive at the remains of a trestle that spanned a bay of Cache Lake.

Track and Tower Trail KM 25

The railway bed forms part of this trail, and the history of the railway is discussed in the trail guide booklet. The remains of several trestles can also be viewed from this excellent trail. It is intriguing to think that during the First World War armed guards stood sentinel on these trestles, to thwart potential saboteurs. Use of this section of the railway was discontinued in 1933.

Highland Backpacking Trail KM 29.7

One can access the old railway bed by walking 2.8 km (1.8 miles) along this trail. At this point the rail bed intersects the Highland Backpacking Trail, and the section leading northeast forms part of the trail.

Airfield KM 30.6

Drive past the Mew Lake Campground office until you reach the "T" junction at the old airfield. The parking lot is to your left. You can access the old railway by walking southeast across the airfield along the Old Railway Bike Trail. After crossing the Madawaska River, you reach the rail bed, now part of the bike trail. You can also travel west on the dirt road that you reach on the far side of the airfield until you come to a side trail of the Track and Tower Trail. Travel along this until you reach Post #15. Here the trail follows the old rail bed.

Rock Lake 7.5 km (6.6 miles) south from KM 40.3

When you arrive at the Rock Lake Campground office you have reached the old railway bed which serves as a road from this point to the parking lot for the Booth's Rock Trail. The last section of that trail also follows the rail bed.

OTHER SITES OF HISTORICAL INTEREST

A few additional points of interest are detailed here.

Frank A. MacDougall Memorial West Gate

Frank MacDougall, a forester and the Park Superintendent from 1931 to 1941, was responsible for introducing the airplane as a tool in fire detection and monitoring of provincial parks. The MacDougall Parkway, the section of Highway 60 between the park boundaries, was named in his honour in 1976. The memorial is located on a rock outside the Information building at the West Gate.

Tote Road and Building Remains KM 7.2

These sites are located along the Whiskey Rapids Trail. The 45 km (28 miles) of tote road extended from Dorset (west of Algonquin) to the north end of Canoe Lake and crossed the Oxtongue River at the Tea Lake Dam. In the late 1800s horse-drawn wagons in summer and sleighs in winter were used to haul supplies. The tote road forms the portion of the trail between Post #10 and the parking lot. Between Posts #9 and #10, the rotting remains of what was either a halfway house or shelters used by river drivers are visible.

Tea Lake Dam KM 8.1

The dam is located on the Oxtongue River at the end of the Tea Lake Dam Picnic Ground. This modern dam, built in 1964, replaces a much earlier wooden version that Tom Thomson, one of Canada's most renowned artists, painted in 1915. It is believed that Thomson's first trip to Algonquin involved a camping trip to this very spot.

James Dickson Memorial KM 20

You will find this memorial along the stairs to the Algonquin Art Centre. Dickson was the provincial land surveyor who, through his recommendations and surveys, was instrumental in the formation of Algonquin Park. At the top of the stairs you will find the Algonquin Art Centre, formerly the Park Museum (1953–1992).

Highland Inn KM 23.5

This site is described in the Cache Lake entry in the OA&PS Railway section (page 126).

Airfield KM 30.6

The Mew Lake Airfield, situated between Mew Lake and Lake of Two Rivers, can be reached by driving past the Mew Lake Campground office until you reach the parking lot on your left (the airfield is straight ahead, and you turn right to go to the Mew Lake Campground).

This extensive open area was cleared in 1935 as an emergency landing strip. Although it has never been used for that purpose, planes have occasionally landed there when short on fuel. It has also been used for a variety of activities, including fire control demonstrations and fly-in breakfasts. Conducted interpretive outings, including bird walks, are currently held here.

McRae Mill Site KM 30.6

Only a few subtle remains identify the site of this former sawmill built in 1931 and last used in 1944. It lies along the Old Railway bed on the far side of the Madawaska River on the south side of the airfield. To reach the site, follow the Old Railway Bike Trail across the airfield and proceed across the Madawaska River bridge until you reach the rail bed. Turn left on the rail bed (still part of the Bike Trail) and follow it to the opening where the mill formerly stood.

Hammer and Sickle KM 35.3

These symbols, along with the year "34", can be discerned on the rock cut just to the east of the lane on the south side of the highway. Highway 60 was built in the mid-1930s, and it has been suggested that these figures were chiselled in the rock by a member of the Communist Party, which had some followers in Canada at that time. For safety reasons, it is wise to park well east of this point, possibly near the entrance to East Beach (KM 35.4), because cars unexpectedly come speeding over the hill to the west.

McRae Mill Site 7.5 km (4.5 miles) south from KM 40.3

The second and more recent sawmill was run by McRae Lumber on this site from 1957 to 1979. To get to the site, travel south on the Rock Lake Road until you reach the campground office. Park here and walk west approximately 0.5 km (0.3 mile) along the gated road, which is part of the Old Railway Bike Trail. The mill site lies only a short distance past the bridge. Either fork on the road will take you into the site.

Vision Pits, Rock Cairns and Pictographs

8 km (5 miles) south from KM 40.3

Of particular interest are some archaeological sites on the west side of Rock Lake directly across from the campground. These can be reached only by water either from the boat launch at the bottom end of the Rock Lake Road or from the beach beside the Booth's Rock Trail parking lot. Please see the Rock Lake entry in "Other Day Trips" (page 138) for details concerning this site.

Barclay Estate 9 km (5.4 miles) south from KM 40.3

This site lies on the Booth's Rock Trail. You can take a shortcut to it by travelling backward on the trail along the old rail bed of the OA&PS Railway. When you turn right at Post #9, you will have reached the grounds of the estate.

The estate was built at the turn of the 20th century by Judge George Barclay, a relative of J.R. Booth, the lumber potentate who built the railway. It was last used in 1953 and all that survives now are some foundations, the gradually disappearing tennis courts and the remnants of the docks.

Alexander Kirkwood Memorial KM 43

Algonquin Park owes its existence to the foresight of Alexander Kirkwood. In 1885 Kirkwood, a chief clerk in the Ontario office of the Ontario Department of Crown Lands, proposed the idea of a park to conserve the forests and protect the headwaters of five major rivers flowing from it. A plaque commemorating Kirkwood's contribution to the formation of what is now Algonquin Provincial Park has been erected on the large rock at the left side of the entrance ramp to the Visitor Centre.

Harkness Memorial 6 km (4miles) north from KM 46.3

Dr. William John Knox Harkness, the man responsible for the establishment of the Harkness Laboratory of Fisheries Research, which is located at this site, is honoured here. The plaque is on a cairn only a short distance past the parking lot on the north side of the Opeongo Store. Just walk along the road (closed to unauthorized vehicles) that hugs the shoreline past the parking lot. The cairn is on the point to the right of the first building you come to.

Dr. Harkness was a professor of limnology at the University of Toronto and was also Chief of the Fish and Wildlife Branch of the Ontario Department of Lands and Forests.

St. Anthony Lumber Company Railway Spur Line KM 52

Take the dirt road running east just south of West Smith Lake. Watch carefully for a trail on the north (left) side of the road, halfway between the highway and the end of this short road. The trail lies on the railway spur line that once ran from Whitney to Opeongo Lake. The line extended north from here to Little McCauley Lake, and then south back to the highway at the north end of Brewer Lake. Short sections of both Highway 60 and the Opeongo Road are now located along parts of the rail bed once used to transport timber. The spur line was built in 1902 and was abandoned in 1926.

The site of a former sawmill is located along this spur line between West Smith and Whitney lakes. However, access could be difficult. Parts of this rail bed are not passable because of erosion and dense tree growth.

Algonquin Logging Museum KM 54.6

This museum exhibits a fascinating assortment of historical logging buildings, structures and equipment chronologically arranged along a scenic trail. While some of the buildings, such as the "camboose" (a log structure with bunks arranged around a large central fireplace), are accurate replicas, others, including two ranger cabins, are actual original buildings transported from their former sites.

Other highlights include a steam locomotive and a replicated log chute and dam. The *William M.*, a steam-warping tug also known as an alligator, combined the functions of a steam boat and a steam winch, and towed log booms across large lakes. It is one of only three still in existence. This unique steam-driven boat could travel both across water by use of paddlewheels and over land by winch and log skids. The road to the museum crosses the St. Anthony Lumber Company Spur Line described in the previous entry.

CANOEING IN THE CORRIDOR

 My favourite way of exploring Algonquin's Highway Corridor is by canoe. The pleasure of silently paddling along a winding river or creek and rounding a bend to encounter a moose or a heron is a true wilderness experience. Regardless of how busy the season may be, if you paddle at daybreak your canoe will frequently be the only one out there! In addition to seeing more wildlife, you'll get the bonus of experiencing the most satisfying time of day. A canoe or kayak also allows you to visit a number of historical sites as well as participate in special interpretive events.

Be aware that each person in a canoe must have a regulation life jacket, now known as a "Personal Flotation Device" (PFD). In addition, some sort of bailing equipment, a spare paddle, a 15 metre (50-foot) length of floating rope, and a PSD (Personal Signalling Device – i.e., a whistle) are currently required. *Canoe Routes of Algonquin Provincial Park* is not only an essential navigational tool but also a wonderful keepsake of the trip.

AVAILABLE SERVICES

 Canoes, kayaks and all associated gear can be rented at the Portage Store (KM 14.1), which delivers canoes to campgrounds, the Opeongo Store (Algonquin Outfitters) (6.2 km/3.9 miles north from KM 46.3), and the Opeongo Outfitters in Whitney, which also delivers canoes into the Park. All three offer complete outfitting services. The Opeongo Store also rents Holby Pedal Boats.

The Portage Store provides guided day outings for which the fee includes all equipment and a lunch. The Opeongo Store offers both guided and unguided excursions to Hailstorm Creek, a fabulous waterway for moose and other wildlife. Fees include all equipment and a lunch. Part of the package includes a water taxi shuttle service, which is also available for canoeists who wish to avoid paddling the immense expanse of Opeongo Lake. Opeongo Outfitters in Whitney also provides a water taxi service.

The Park Interpretive Program offers free guided outings on which participants bring their own equipment (frequently rented from one of the stores) and a lunch. These casual outings offer some canoeing instruction but focus on the natural and human history encountered on the outing.

The Canoe Centres on both Canoe and Opeongo lakes sell permits and provide free information and advice for Interior canoeing and camping. *Canoe Routes of Algonquin Provincal Park* map-brochures are available at these centres as well as at the gates and museums.

RECOMMENDED SHORT TRIPS

The Highway Corridor is a doorway into the Park Interior, with a number of different access points from which to start overnight trips. In this chapter, however, only excursions that take a day or less will be discussed. For a description of Interior highlights requiring longer trips refer to "The Park Interior" (page 199).

The following trips are all quite short, most taking about half a day, but several could be extended into a full day or longer if desired. It is always a good idea to pack some food and beverages even for a half-day trip. Please remember, cans and bottles are prohibited from the Park Interior, and Interior permits must be obtained if you intend to camp overnight.

Costello Creek is a typical Algonquin waterway to explore by canoe.

The Oxtongue River KM14.1 or KM 3

This is a beautiful river for canoeing, with a steady gentle current that presents little challenge. As you meander around its twists and turns, you will see great beds of swaying bulrush waving their stems beneath the surface. The spruce and firs that line its shores harbour northern birds such as boreal chickadees and black-backed woodpeckers. The "quick-three-beers" whistles of olive-sided flycatchers follow you around each bend, and the raucous chatter of red squirrels scolds you for your intrusion. Great blue herons flush ahead, only to land and then flush again, while common mergansers spatter across the river surface.

The many options for accessing this river include starting at the Portage Store on Canoe Lake (KM 14.1) and paddling down through Bonita into Tea Lake. Once on the river, you will encounter only a couple of short portages (trails on which a canoe is carried between bodies of water, in Algonquin identified by black and yellow signs depicting a canoe being carried) between the Western Uplands Backpacking Trail and the starting point.

Another option, one that I frequently use, is to launch at the Western Uplands Backpacking Trail (KM 3) and paddle west to the first portage at Lower Twin Falls. About halfway down this route there is a short stretch of shallow water (shown as rapids on the *Canoe Routes of Algonquin Provincial Park* map-brochure) that you may wish to walk your canoe through. Old sneakers or "Crocs" (at least so I'm told) are ideal for this enterprise. You can also carry your canoe around the south side.

It is sometimes possible to float it over the rocks when the water is high, but my experience is that this is not usually the case.

Watch for the beautiful trumpet-shaped structures of net-spinning caddisflies in the upper part of these gentle rapids. The current enters the net's large opening and passes through to the narrow end where the larva lies in wait for minute particles of food to arrive. Also watch for the bright green mounds of freshwater sponges, colonial animals that also filter their food from the current.

The portage around Lower Twin Falls is an excellent place to end this part of the trip. The rocks along the pretty little falls, which are really more a rapids, are excellent sites for picnic lunches.

If you feel like continuing downriver, you could take another short portage less than 50 metres (550 yards) farther along. This is a tricky one, since the banks are steep and the current here is strong. If you plan to continue, watch for this awkward portage and be prepared in advance to hug the south (left) shoreline as you approach the rapids.

If you are travelling with a small group and have the luxury of a second vehicle, you may wish to leave one just past the park boundary, where a short portage brings you to the highway from the river. This allows you to paddle downstream for the entire trip. Be aware of the extra distance involved and that the second portage west of the Western Uplands Backpacking Trail is only about halfway to the Park boundary.

MAP 6
HIGHWAY CORRIDOR KM 46–KM 56

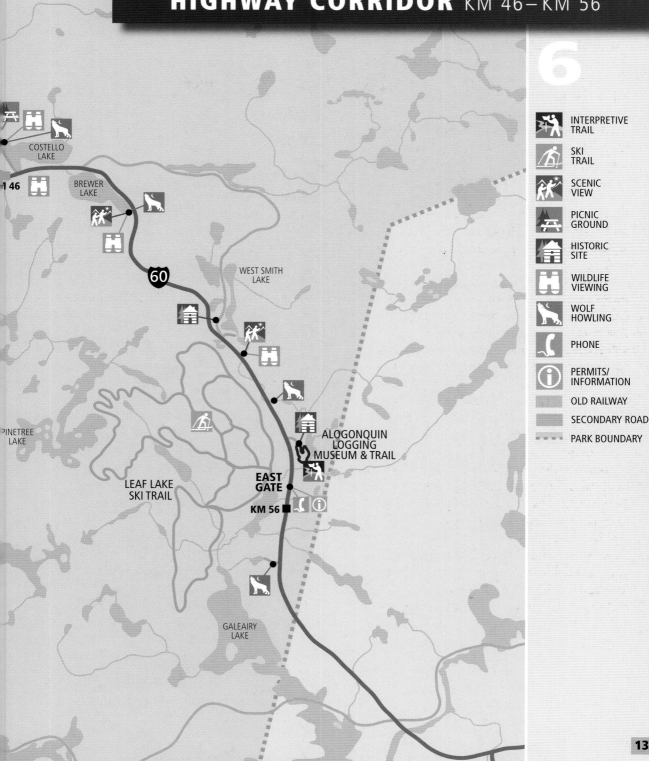

6

COSTELLO LAKE

KM 46

BREWER LAKE

60

WEST SMITH LAKE

PINETREE LAKE

LEAF LAKE SKI TRAIL

EAST GATE

ALOGONQUIN LOGGING MUSEUM & TRAIL

KM 56

GALEAIRY LAKE

INTERPRETIVE TRAIL

SKI TRAIL

SCENIC VIEW

PICNIC GROUND

HISTORIC SITE

WILDLIFE VIEWING

WOLF HOWLING

PHONE

PERMITS/ INFORMATION

OLD RAILWAY

SECONDARY ROAD

PARK BOUNDARY

133

The Madawaska River KM 35.4

This trip is one of my favourites. The Madawaska is a delightful winding river along which I have encountered plenty of wildlife. The Madawaska also holds a special place in my heart since I spent time at its source (Source Lake) in the summer and grew up near its mouth (Arnprior, where it joins the Ottawa River). I generally put my canoe in at the boat launch at the Lake of Two Rivers East Beach (KM 35.4). From there I paddle down to Whitefish Lake and back. Of course, one can make this a longer trip if desired, for it is an easy journey to Rock Lake from Whitefish. If you are camping at Pog Lake Campground, you could start paddling from the lake, since the Madawaska flows through it. There is only one very short portage around Pog Lake dam.

I have often met moose, river otters, great blue herons, common mergansers, muskrats, beavers and American black ducks on this river. There are some excellent stretches that are bordered by northern woods where boreal chickadees and gray jays are sometimes found.

Another attraction is the historic OA&PS Railway, which follows the river for much of this route. Watch for the old culverts, in particular the one constructed of stones, which you pass on the right (west) side of the river between Lake of Two Rivers and Pog Lake Dam. The more modern circular culvert has contained a beaver dam.

Also watch the water for the abundant green growth of freshwater sponge that covers submerged rocks and logs, particularly just below the dam. At times it resembles finger-like extensions; at others it appears as circular patches on the rocks. Be sure to pick up a piece (carefully, so as not to tip the canoe), to feel its peculiar texture and sniff the curious aroma. If you are paddling along this route in late summer, keep your eyes peeled for the bizarre white blooms of turtlehead, an uncommon flower in Algonquin, which peeks out from the shores below the dam.

At the point where the Madawaska River meets the bay at the north end of Whitefish Lake (where the group campground is situated), you will come across a shallow area on the left side of creek. Look carefully for snapping turtles that lie submerged, with only their snouts projecting out of the water.

Once you reach Whitefish Lake, you might enjoy lunch and a swim at the large sand beach at the Group Campground. Alternatively, you can paddle over to the rocky points directly across the bay or along the east shore. From there you can either continue down Whitefish Lake or return. The top end of Whitefish Lake is really a river, but it eventually widens before reaching Rock Lake. If you are travelling with a few others, consider leaving a vehicle at Rock Lake and making this a one-way trip. Note, however, that motorboats are permitted on Whitefish and Rock lakes.

The Madawaska River is ideal for invigorating day trips by canoe or kayak.

Costello Creek 3–6.2 km (2–4 miles) north from KM 46.3

Even though this trip is shorter than the above-mentioned routes and follows a public road for a short distance, Costello Creek remains one of my favourite Algonquin waterways. Not only have I seen numerous animals on this creek but the scenery is often so stunning that I am compelled to stop paddling and drift, absorbed by the surrounding beauty. Several of the photographs in *Moose Country*, *Algonquin Seasons* and *Algonquin Souvenir* were taken along this creek.

The best access is from the boat launch the Opeongo Store. Just past the store there are parking lots where you can leave your vehicle. Motorboats are allowed on Opeongo Lake but are prohibited from entering Costello Creek. On the tiny island just south of the boat launch, there is a sign to this effect.

Try starting your trip at the crack of dawn. At this time there is usually little wind, and wildlife, unlike humans, are at their most active. Paddle south from the docks into the narrowing of Opeongo that becomes Costello Creek. On the left side is an open floating bog where the carnivorous bog plants sundew and pitcher-plant can easily be found. A number of beaver lodges, some active, are also visible along the edge of this bog mat.

When you enter the narrow channel before the creek opens up again, watch out for a couple of large submerged rocks that could scrape the bottom of your canoe. There is a deep channel here, so with a little bit of care you can avoid these potential obstacles.

After the narrows, the creek winds through a fairly extensive bog mat punctuated with cattail clumps. Great blue herons frequently fly up just ahead of your canoe and land a couple of bends farther along. Sometimes you will paddle around a bend and meet up with an American bittern. Although bitterns will fly to escape, they occasionally point their beaks into the air and freeze, relying on their breast stripes to blend in with the vegetation and make them invisible. Their strange song, which resembles a stake being driven into soft mud, can often be heard along the creek.

Dead trees, resulting from raised water levels in the lake, provide homes and perches for a variety of birds. The "quick-three-beer" whistles of olive-sided flycatchers taunt you from the tops of these snags, while the sleepy "sweet-sweet-Canada-Canada-Canada" of the white-throated sparrow drifts from the spruces. Tree swallows twitter and eastern kingbirds angrily buzz over your canoe as you float by.

As soon as you pass through the narrows, the overwhelming beauty of this route becomes apparent. The open expanse of bog mat is bordered by a neat fringe of black spruce and tamarack. These trees start out being quite tall near the high ground but shrink in stature as they approach the open creek. Farther along, a rugged cliff towers to the east. This dramatic scenery is transformed into a wonderland in August when glowing morning mists swirl into the warming rays of the rising sun.

Moose feed in the creek in early summer and I have also observed deer along the Costello Creek shoreline. Otters inhabit the creek and mink hunt along it. Watch for droppings of these animals in the crevice of the huge boulder that you eventually paddle around. Just past this boulder is a small "island" on the right that is a wonderful spot for a rest or a lunch break. Past the rock lies the Opeongo Road. If you wish to continue along the creek, you can portage the canoe over the road or, if the water is high, you can paddle under it through the culvert – unless beavers have dammed it up.

If you walk along the road south from the

culvert, on your left you will see a footpath leading up the hillside. Large scattered rocks along the hill make good seats for lunch and offer a view of the creek you just travelled.

Other Day Trips

While the aforementioned are my three favourite routes, a number of other trips are possible. These, however, include lakes on which motorboats are allowed (none of the above routes have motorboat activity, apart from the very end of the Madawaska route in Whitefish Lake and the start of the Costello Creek route at Opeongo Lake). Also, with their larger expanses of water, these lake routes can be a challenge on windy days. However, a number of fascinating historical sites are situated along some of these routes, so if the day is calm, you may want to try them.

The Tom Thomson memorial cairn overlooking Canoe Lake can only be accessed by water.

Canoe Lake KM 14.1

Canoe Lake is one of the busiest lakes in the Park, largely because it is the major launching point for canoe trips into the Interior. Motorboats churn its waters, taking leaseholders to their cottages or carrying people and supplies to the children's camps (Wapomeo and Ahmek) situated on the lake. I would recommend paddling on Canoe Lake as early as possible in the morning when very few motorboats are out and about. But you may meet a few on your return trip.

Most sites of interest are located at the north end of the lake. On the north-central point you will see a rather incongruous totem pole. It marks the spot where a cairn, well worth visiting, was erected in September, 1917, to honour the Canadian artist Tom Thomson. A small dock offers a place to access the short footpaths leading up to it. This monument was erected by Thomson's friends, including artists who later became known as the Group of Seven. The epitaph on the bronze plaque, composed and beautifully designed by J.E.H. MacDonald, is so moving that I feel compelled to print it here in case you don't get a chance to visit the cairn.

To the memory of Tom Thomson, artist, woodsman and guide, who was drowned in Canoe Lake, July 8, 1917. He lived humbly but passionately with the wild. It made him brother to all untamed things of nature. It drew him apart and revealed itself to him wonderfully. It sent him out from the woods only to show these revelations through his art, and it took him to itself at last.

Thomson drowned in Canoe Lake under suspicious circumstances that have fuelled much conjecture and inspired more than one book, play and movie. Whether he drowned accidentally or was killed is ultimately of little or no consequence. Let it suffice that the magnificence of Algonquin captured his heart, and its beauty lives on through his art.

On the far shore directly west of the cairn lies the former townsite of Mowat. Established by the Gilmour Lumber Company in 1893, Mowat was also the site of the first Park Headquarters. By 1896 at least 600 men lived here. When the mill closed down in 1900 following the bankruptcy of the Gilmour Company, the thriving lumber town soon fell quiet. Apparently the bankruptcy was at least in part due to a failed and incredibly costly scheme to transport logs from Mowat to Trenton. Logs were floated down Canoe Lake and the Oxtongue River to Lake of Bays. An "alligator" would then pull them in booms to Baysville, from where they were dragged in a long chain-and-trough system overland to Raven Lake. They were finally floated down the Trent River system to Lake Ontario. Unfortunately, the journey was so arduous that by the time the logs made it to the end they were in such poor shape that they were practically unusable.

Mowat soon became a popular tourist destination, and Mowat Lodge, which opened in 1913, became Thomson's summer headquarters. The busy atmosphere at Mowat was once again doomed, however. The lodge burned down in 1920, was rebuilt at a new location, and then burned down again in 1930. The once-thriving town of Mowat gradually deteriorated into a virtual ghost town. North from the Mowat town site lies the rail bed of the OA&PS Railway, accessible by taking either of the two branches of the lake. The left branch leads you up picturesque Potter Creek to the railway bridge. The right branch eventually takes you to the old rail bed along the bottom of Joe Lake, after a short portage around Joe Lake Dam. Two major buildings used to stand in this area: Joe Lake Station was located along the rail bed near the bridge just above the dam, while the Algonquin Hotel, built in 1908, was on the hill between the dam and the rail bed on the west side of the waterway.

Smoke Lake KM 14.1

Nominigan Lodge formerly graced the point on the north side of the large bay approximately a third of the way down the east side of the lake. (As an extra point of reference, its site is due north of Molly Island.) The lodge was built in 1913 and accommodated guests who arrived at Algonquin Park Station on Cache Lake. A horse-drawn taxi would deliver visitors from the train station to the lodge for a dollar per person. The lodge was dismantled in 1977.

The main item of historical interest still visible now is the site of a log chute on the creek on the east side of the portage between Smoke and Ragged lakes. This wooden chute, typical of those built throughout Algonquin from the mid-1800s to the early 1900s, was vital for transporting logs over damaging rapids and waterfalls. All that remains of this chute, built in 1896, is a scattering of rotten timbers and planks.

Rock Lake 8 km (5 miles) south from KM 40.3

You can gain access to Rock Lake from the boat launch at the bottom end of the Rock Lake Road or from the beach beside the Booth's Rock Trail parking lot.

Of particular interest are some archaeological sites on the west side of the lake, across from the campground. As you paddle along the west shore, heading south from where the Madawaska River enters the lake, you will come to a series of cottages. Just before the first cottage you will see an opening with foundations of a former building. Land here. If you walk north from the west edge of the clearing and parallel to the shoreline, you will soon enter a group of hemlocks (there may be orange flagging tape marking the route). Among the trees are a number of shallow pits, difficult to find because they are obscured by years of debris falling into them. These are known as "vision pits." Early Algonkians would apparently lie in these small depressions, possibly for days on end, until they experienced a vision. Please do not disturb the site in any way.

While the pits may not be impressive to see, the rock piles that these natives built in memory of their visions certainly are. To locate these, climb the steep hillside in a south-westerly direction on about a 45-degree angle from the pits. Orange flagging tape may indicate the route to this site. After climbing for several minutes, you should reach a plateau below a second rise. Along this plateau are situated the moss-covered rock piles, which stand about a 1 metres (3 feet) tall. Waist-high vegetation has made the piles difficult to see in recent years so it might involve some diligent searching to locate them. Please respect this sacred site and, as with the vision pits,

do not disturb the cairns.

The rail bed of the OA&PS Railway follows the eastern shoreline from the campground down to the large point about halfway along the east side of the lake. The remains of the Barclay Estate buildings, described in "Other Historic Sites" (page 128), are found on this point, and the remnants of the large docks are visible on its south side.

On the west shore directly across from the point lies another archaeological site. Native pictographs were once visible on the cliff faces, but over time they have almost entirely faded away.

Sunday Creek KM 42.7

This route follows a winding creek to a couple of small lakes south of Highway 60. You can put in right from the highway, but it may be wise to park across the road in the Spruce Bog Boardwalk parking area.

Sunday Creek is a pretty, meandering creek that takes you to Norway and Fork lakes. At least two beaver dams block the creek, so be prepared to step out of your canoe and drag it over them. In addition to a grand view of a bog and boreal forest along part of the route, you will also be treated to a view of the Visitor Centre on the ridge to the east of the creek.

Norway and Fork lakes are pretty bodies of water on which you might come across moose. If you are here in late summer, be sure to try wolf howling along this route, for wolves regularly travel through this area and seem more than willing to answer back.

THE EAST SIDE

Although it has become busier in recent years, the East Side of Algonquin sees substantially fewer visitors than does the Highway 60 Corridor. Yet it offers many of the same services, including a public campground, interpretive trails and facilities, and a number of access routes to the Interior. Just outside the Park is an outfitter that delivers canoe and kayak rentals into this part of Algonquin.

The rugged landscape and coniferous forests give this side of the Park a distinctive beauty and feel that are quite different from those of the western uplands. Pine and poplar forests dominate the landscape, and many of the plants and animals they support are either more common here or are not found at all on the West Side. Cardinal-flower and poison ivy, for example, both virtually non-existent in the Highway Corridor, are relatively common on the East Side. This part of Algonquin offers excellent viewing opportunities for animals, including white-tailed deer, moose, black bear, and eastern wolf, and many historical as well as natural history sites can be reached with reasonable ease.

The Barron Canyon is a geological fault that occurred more than a billion years ago.

Access is achieved from Highway 17 just west of Pembroke at the first Petawawa exit. Turn south on Renfrew County Road 26 (opposite the Airport sign) and then almost immediately turn right on the Barron Canyon Road (Renfrew County Road 28). This road is paved for the next 9 km (5.6 miles). Starting from the point where the pavement ends, every kilometre is marked. This numbering system, which was devised for communication of location between drivers of logging trucks, continues to the end of public access at Lake Travers, which is 72 km (45 miles) from this point. I will indicate the location of points of interest in the same way as I did for the Highway Corridor. For example, the Sand Lake gate is 18 km (11 miles) along unpaved road, and its location will be given as KM 18.

There is a short access road leading to Mallard and Sec lakes at KM 15.2. You must obtain a permit if you wish to visit these lakes. As is the rule for all of Algonquin, travellers must obtain and display permits for all day use and for camping in the Achray Campground and Park Interior. These can be purchased at the Sand Lake gate, which is less than 3 km (1.8 miles) past the exit to Mallard and Sec lakes.

From the gate, the Barron Canyon Road extends another 54 km (33.5 miles) to Lake Travers. Two main public access roads lead off the Barron Canyon Road: one at KM 24 (leading to McManus Lake) and another at KM 37.8 (leading to Achray on Grand Lake). There are two shorter public roads at KM 67 and KM 70.3. You will also come across a number of logging roads running off both sides of the main road but these are closed to public vehicular travel and are posted to this effect.

The roads in this part of Algonquin are unpaved and windy, so drive slowly. As they become quite dusty during dry periods, you might be wise to roll up your windows when you see an approaching vehicle.

Since the East Side lacks gasoline and food services, make sure that your vehicle is filled up and that all your food requirements are satisfied before you arrive. However, the Algonquin Portage Store (613-735-1795) is located only 21 km (13 miles) east of the Sand Lake gate and it offers sandwiches, a few groceries, complete outfitting services, accommodation, pay showers and gasoline.

INTERPRETIVE WALKING TRAILS

 As along Highway 60, trail guide booklets are available in dispensers at the beginning of the interpretive walking trails (the exception being the Jack Pine Trail, which has no trail guide booklet). They are also available at the Sand Lake gate and the Achray office or can be purchased from the Friends of Algonquin (address on page 215).

The red of cardinal-flowers catches the eye of the hummingbird, which, unlike most insects, can see that colour.

MAP 7
EAST SIDE

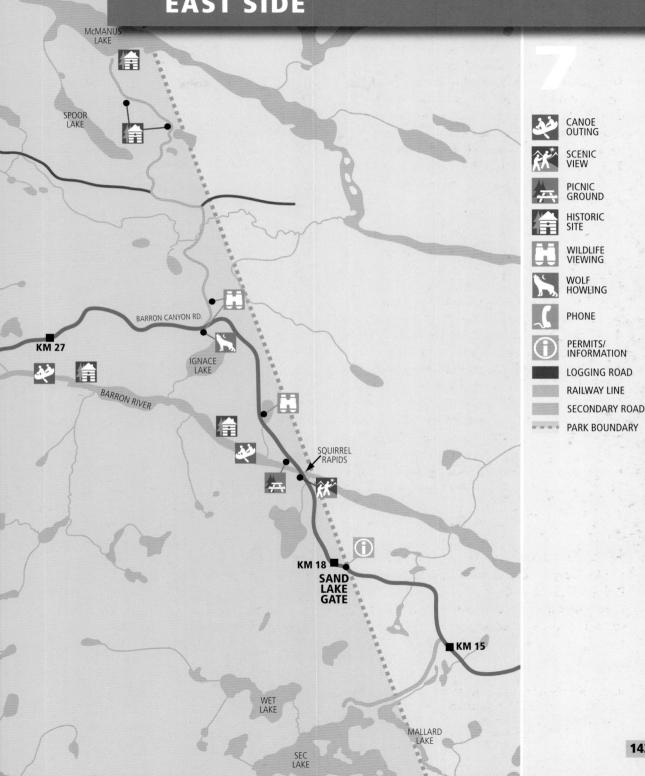

7

MCMANUS LAKE

SPOOR LAKE

BARRON CANYON RD.

KM 27

BARRON RIVER

IGNACE LAKE

SQUIRREL RAPIDS

KM 18

SAND LAKE GATE

KM 15

WET LAKE

MALLARD LAKE

SEC LAKE

Legend

🛶 CANOE OUTING

SCENIC VIEW

🏕 PICNIC GROUND

🏚 HISTORIC SITE

🔭 WILDLIFE VIEWING

🐺 WOLF HOWLING

☎ PHONE

ⓘ PERMITS/ INFORMATION

▬ LOGGING ROAD

▬ RAILWAY LINE

▬ SECONDARY ROAD

- - - PARK BOUNDARY

Barron Canyon Trail KM 28.9

The East Side boasts a unique trail that is one of the most impressive in all of Algonquin, possibly in all of eastern Canada. As its name suggests, the Barron Canyon Trail visits a magnificent gorge along the Barron River. The trail, only 1.5 km (1 mile) long, leads to the top of the ancient canyon, which rises dramatically 100 metres (330 feet) above the river.

This has always been one of my favourite places in Algonquin. The canyon is as awe-inspiring from below as it is from above. The walls are painted orange xanthoria with elegant sunburst lichen, and many unusual ferns and other rare plants cling to the steep surfaces. Noisy common ravens nest on cliff ledges and yellow-bellied flycatchers hiccup from the cool cedars deep in the canyon.

Far below the cliff top, the Barron River is a tranquil ribbon of water. In earlier times, however, it was a raging glacial waterway estimated to have contained the volume of a thousand Niagaras. Long after the glaciers had retreated farther north, the icy water draining through the gorge maintained a cold environment in the canyon. Evidence of this is found in the several species of northern plants and four types of Arctic crustaceans that reside within the confines of the canyon, all relics of populations that were widespread during the last retreat of the glaciers.

The rocks of the canyon are part of the same ancient Canadian Shield that is the backbone of Algonquin. A great geological fault, a crack in the ancient rock, was responsible for the creation of the canyon, which continues to change today. Continual erosion and crumbing of the cliffs,

Canoeing through the Barron Canyon offers a perspective very different from the cliff-top trail.

caused largely by the action of frost and tree roots, create the rubble of rocks known as talus that lies at the base of the walls.

A strange combination of birds thrives in the canyon. Along the shores of the canyon, boreal-dwelling yellow-bellied flycatchers perch above wetland-loving common yellowthroats. Red-tailed hawks soar with common ravens and turkey vultures on the thermals rising from the gorge. The soft trills of dark-eyed juncos join the abrupt inflections of eastern phoebes echoing through the canyon.

In addition to supporting an interesting mixture of life, the Barron Canyon offers breathtaking views. Because the trail visits the edge of a cliff, please make sure that your children and pets are under physical control when you explore it.

Berm Lake Trail from Achray, 5 km (3 miles) south from KM 37.8

The Berm Lake Trail begins at the end of the large parking area to your left as you approach the Achray office. This beautiful trail takes you around Berm Lake through a typical East Side pine forest, the ecology of which is discussed in the trail guide booklet.

With the fragrance of pines filling the air and carpets of lichens and mosses bordering it, this trail is a delight to walk. In early June the delicate pouches of pink lady's-slippers add yet another element of form and colour to the landscape.

This trail is part of the Achray Trail System, and you can extend your walk by connecting with the Eastern Pines Backpacking Trail. If you do, be sure you have with you the map-brochure *Backpacking Trails of Algonquin Provincial Park* (available at the Achray office and Sand Lake gate). There are some spectacular sites on this backpacking trail, including a dramatic glacial boulder garden and a magnificent waterfall.

The Jack Pine Trail from Achray, 5 km (3 miles) south of KM 37.8

This short 1.6 km (1-mile) round trip leads from the southeast end of the Achray Campground to the site on Grand Lake where ground-breaking Canadian artist Tom Thomson, who drowned in Canoe Lake in 1917, sketched one of his most famous works, *The Jack Pine*. The trail travels along an old road through a mixed pine forest to a rocky outcrop covered in jack pines. Unlike all other interpretive trails in Algonquin, this one has no accompanying trail guide booklet; however, at the site there is an interpretive display. Just to the east of the point is one of the finest sand beaches in Algonquin.

BACKPACKING TRAILS

 The Eastern Pines Backpacking Trail is a fantastic trail ranging from 6 to 17.2 km (3.7 to 10.6 miles) if the optional but not-to-be-missed side trip to High Falls is taken. While there are a number of Interior campsites, which can be and perhaps should be reserved, the entire trail can be walked in a single day. Much of the trail follows relatively level ground and, since there is just one large hill to climb, a one-day trek is feasible as long as you allow yourself plenty of time for breathers. If you choose this option, be sure to get an early morning start and bring along plenty of water and food.

The trail skirts several lakes, including Johnston, on which great blue herons and osprey currently nest. One loop of the trail visits a collection of gigantic boulders left 10,000 years ago by the retreating glaciers. Another loop brings you to stunning High Falls, which lies on the Barron River just below Stratton Lake. The views of the cascading water, most impressive in spring, make this alone worth the trip. Many people take advantage of the natural water slide for a cooling swim. This waterfall can also be accessed by canoe or kayak, either from the Barron River or via Grand and Stratton lakes.

The Eastern Pines Backpacking Trail is detailed in the map-brochure *The Backpacking Trails of Algonquin Provincial Park*, available at the Sand Lake gate and the Achray office, or through the Friends of Algonquin Park.

WALKING TRAILS

 As there is an interpretive display board at the site where Tom Thomson sketched one of his most famous works, the Jack Pine Trail is considered to be one of the Park's Interpretive Trails, and is discussed on page 146.

Railway Bed Achray
The abandoned Canadian National Railway rail bed, now without its steel rails and ties, can be walked both east and west from the Achray campground.

INTERPRETIVE PROGRAM

Currently an interpretive program is offered on weekends in the summer. Evening programs are held in the building on the north side of the main parking area, and interpretive walks and Algonquin for Kids programs are conducted on nearby trails. Events are listed in the weekly flyer *This Week in Algonquin, Achray Campground*, which is posted at the Sand Lake gate and Achray Campground bulletin boards, and is available at the Achray office.

Outside In is an interpretive facility inside a log cabin used by Tom Thomson during his stint as a fire ranger at Achray in 1916. The whereabouts of the original sign, which was painted by Thomson, but was spelled "Out-Side-In"), is currently unknown. Exhibits inside the building explain Thomson's role in Algonquin's history and examine the ecology of the East Side of Algonquin.

FACILITIES

 Unlike the Highway Corridor, there are no restaurants, lodges or outfitting services in the East Side of Algonquin. The Sand Lake gate (613-732-1313) sells permits and park publications. The Achray office sells ice, snacks, drinks, and park publications. It also has a handful of canoes and kayaks that can be rented by campers. The Algonquin Portage Store, 21 km (13 miles) east of the Sand Lake gate, offers full outfitting services, including shuttles and canoe pick-up and drop-off.

PICNIC GROUNDS

 A number of picnic tables are available beside the Barron River at Squirrel Rapids (KM 20.3). There is also a parking lot for canoe trippers who launch from this site.

At Achray there are also excellent places to have lunch, with picnic tables and barbecue stands situated to the west of the office and boat launch.

In addition, the drive-in camping spot at Pretty Lake (KM 54.5) is a fine spot to eat – if the site is not occupied.

CAMPGROUNDS

Achray Campground 5 km (3 miles) south from KM 37.8

 With extensive pale sand beaches and dramatic hills that line the far shore of Grand Lake, Achray Campground, the sole campground in the entire East Side, is arguably the most beautiful one in all of Algonquin. At night choruses of whip-poor-wills and common loons serenade campers. It is intriguing to know that Tom Thomson, who stayed in the Outside In log cabin, now the interpretive facility, admired and sketched the same sensational scenery that captivates us today.

The campground lacks showers and laundry facilities but has flush toilets. Its superb beaches and splendid scenery, however, more than make up for the lack of a few conveniences. Some sites in this campground are designated dog-free, and all sites are designated radio-free. One yurt is available by reservation only (1-888-688-7275).

Apart from canoeing into Interior campsites, which are plentiful in the Grand Lake/Stratton Lake region, there is one alternative to camping at Achray Campground. There is a campsite on Pretty Lake (KM 54.5) that can be accessed by car. In order to camp here, however, one must comply with the can and bottle ban, as this is classified as an Interior campsite. Since this site lies directly beside the Lake Travers Road, noise from the occasional passing car can be a drawback, although this sound generally dissipates after sunset.

The hills bordering Gand Lake are capped with red oaks and poplars, easily distinguishable in autumn by their colours.

WILDLIFE-VIEWING AREAS

Barron Canyon Road offers many excellent opportunities for wildlife viewing. Most of Algonquin's larger animals can be seen along the 54 km (33.5 miles) of road between the gate and Lake Travers. Certain species, such as porcupine, black bear, and white-tailed deer, are more commonly encountered here than on the Park's West Side.

Most of the following animals can be found anywhere along Barron Canyon Road. A few of the better locations for viewing each species are offered, and tips that might increase your chances of finding these animals are given in "Observing Wildlife" (page 47).

Moose

Moose can be seen between the Sand Lake gate and Lake Travers and are occasionally encountered along the road leading to the Park. In June and early July, when moose are feeding on sodium-rich aquatic plants, any pond is worth checking. The following sites usually provide viewing opportunities.

■ KM 21.4

The pond on the east side of the road is worth taking a look at. A couple of short footpaths lead through the pines to the edge of the water.

■ KM 36.4

A dirt road leading off to the north (the right) leads to a pond that at the time of writing was occupied by beaver. The pond is less than a kilometre along the road, on your left. Although the road is closed to unauthorized vehicles, visitors may walk it.

■ KM 37.8

The Achray Trail System, 5 km (3 miles) south of KM 37.8, begins at the far end of the large

parking area to your left, just before the Achray Campground, and consists of the Berm Lake Trail and the Eastern Pines Backpacking Trail. You might spot moose from anywhere along these trails, which lead to Berm and Johnston lakes. The boggy south end of Berm Lake is particularly worth a look.

■ KM 44

A point on the road offers an excellent view of the west end of a small lake. I have occasionally seen moose feeding in that lake, particularly along the opposite shore.

■ KM 48.3

The large pond on the south side of the road has one of the best summer feeding spots for moose along this road. In earlier years, as many as a dozen have been seen at one time, but at the time of writing there are fewer moose (perhaps due in part to Native hunting), and the pond contains less water. However, it is still worth checking. A short path leads through the pines to a fine vantage point.

■ Pretty Lake KM 54.5

Moose are sometimes seen feeding along the west side of this scenic lake.

■ KM 69.4

The "closed" road leading north brings you to a large opening where a sawmill was formerly situated. (As with all of the Park's "closed" roads, you may walk along them but not drive.) However, it is a pleasant walk (1.5 km/1 mile) through a jack pine forest. A little farther along, to your left, will be a short road leading to a marsh in which moose feed. They can also be found in the former mill site, browsing small trees. Watch for their tracks on the road that loops around the site.

- **KM 70.3**

  Follow the paved road in a short distance, and then take the branch that leads to the right. Moose often feed in the very large pond at the end of the road. Formerly there was a bank of radio telescope dishes at this site.

- **KM 72**

  Moose can occasionally be seen grazing in the pond on the west side of the road.

White-tailed Deer

White-tailed deer are seen on the Barron Canyon Road, particularly in late spring and early summer. The section between the Sand Lake gate and the hydro line (KM 49.9) offers especially good opportunities. As deer often drink at sunrise at the edges of ponds and streams, you might encounter them at any of the locations given for moose. The hydro line and the abandoned mill site at Lake Travers 1.5 km (1 mile) north from KM 69.4 are both good feeding areas.

Black Bear

There are two peak times for encountering black bears along the roadside on the East Side. The first is in early spring (late April and May) when bears are seeking fresh grasses and sedges. The second is in mid-summer (mid-July to early August) when they are dining on blueberries and other fruit in open areas. I have had good luck in seeing black bears between KM 20 and KM 50. In particular, the following areas have been good for viewing bears:

- **Achray Road** KM 37.8

  In late evening or around dawn, bears are occasionally seen on this 5 km (3-mile) road. If you walk only a few metres into the woods along the west side of the Achray Road between 0.6 and 0.8 km (around half a mile)

from where you first turned onto this road, you will find some large American beech trees with excellent bear claw scars on the trunks, left by bears climbing the trees to get beechnuts in the fall.

- **The logging road** leading south from KM 45.9

  This has been a good area for bears in the past. If you walk a short distance along it, you will arrive at a few open areas where bears come to eat the fruit of berry-producing plants.

- **Barron Canyon Road,** just before the 50 KM

  I have seen bears where the hydro line crosses the road on numerous occasions in summer when the berries are ripe, especially on the south side.

Mouth-watering and nutritious blueberries are a late-summer staple of the omnivorous black bear.

Eastern Wolves

I have found that this part of Algonquin offers excellent opportunities to hear – and occasionally see – wolves. Several wolf packs have territories that include parts of Barron Canyon Road and they regularly travel along the road in all seasons.

This habit provides us with important clues as to where to listen or howl. Wolf droppings are distinctive and stand out against the light colour of sand. The droppings, also known as scat, are generally black and are full of their prey's hair. Fresh droppings look moist and won't be covered in dust from passing vehicles. On cold mornings extremely fresh scat has steam rising from it. On wet sand or fresh snow, wolf tracks are also a good clue to the presence of wolves. Whenever you encounter a fresh sign, try howling (refer to "Observing Wildlife," page 47). You may be rewarded for your efforts.

Over the years I have observed wolves at the following locations:

- **McManus Lake Road** KM 24
  Try howling at the junction of this road and the Barron Canyon Road. Also try approximately 4 km (2.5 miles) down this road toward McManus Lake.

Wolves often cross roads, or even travel along them.

- **KM 30**
  Wolves frequently hunt in this vicinity and along the Barron River, just south of here.

- **Hydro Line** KM 49.9
  The logging road that passes west of here is travelled by wolves, as is the road that follows along the hydro line.

- **Pretty Lake** KM 54.5
  This area has traditionally been good for locating wolves. I have fond memories of camping on this lake and having wolves howl from the far shore all through the night. They can also be heard howling near Francis Lake, the lake just west of Pretty.

- **KM 61**
  In the creek system just north of KM 61, I have come across wolves several times.

- **KM 62 to KM 69**
  This section of road, which passes through the jack pine flats, has traditionally been one of the best wolf-spotting areas on the East Side and possibly in all of Algonquin. While you might encounter wolves anywhere along this stretch, KM 66 is the best place to stop. This is the highest point on the flats, and sound carries a phenomenally long way here.

- **KM 69.4**
  Try howling where the "closed" road heads north from the Barron Canyon Road. If you feel energetic, try at the abandoned mill site clearing described in the next entry.

- **The Mill Site** 1.5 km (1 mile) north of KM 69.4
  Wolves often travel through this open site, and in winter can be seen from this vantage point crossing Lake Travers.

Red Fox

Red foxes are usually easily located, since they hunt along the roadsides, particularly at night. You might find rather tame foxes in a number of places along this route. Although their tameness is usually due to frequent contact with people, it is always best to be cautious and keep your distance. Here are some possible fox-spotting points along the Barron Canyon Road.

- **KM 37.8**
  Since foxes often den near the turn-off to Achray, both adults and young are commonly seen in this vicinity from late April through summer. They are frequently spotted along the Achray Road, particularly the short stretch of road south of the junction with Barron Canyon Road.

- **KM 62 to KM 72**
  This part of the road passes through a sandy plateau covered in jack pine. Excellent den sites can be found in the sandbanks all through this area. In particular, the stretch of road near Lake Travers often affords good viewing.

- **The Mill Site** 1.5 km (1 mile) north from KM 69.4 Foxes not only hunt but also occasionally den in this open sandy area.

Red foxes, which often den in sandy areas nearby, can be spotted along the Barron Canyon Road.

Beaver

Being laden with creeks and ponds, the Barron Canyon Road is excellent for observing beavers right from the road. Be aware that beavers occasionally vanish from a site, so that ponds occupied at the time of writing may be vacant during your visit, and new colonies may have arisen in currently unoccupied locations. An active site will exhibit freshly cut sticks and newly placed mud on the dam or lodge. At the time of writing, the following sites supported active beaver colonies:

- **Pond** at KM 21.4

- **Forbes Creek,** at KM 40.1

- **Forbes Creek,** at KM 42.2 to 42.7

- **The small lake** at KM 43.2
  Scan for the familiar "V" of a beaver swimming across this lake. While spectacular sunsets can often be enjoyed from this point, the next location is usually better for beaver observation.

- **The small lake** at KM 44
  Beavers are commonly seen at this end of the lake in the evening.

- **The pond** at KM 45.9
  This pond was colonized by beavers in 1992.

- **The pond** at KM 48.3
  Although better for moose viewing than for spying beaver, this pond still worth checking.

- **The small pond** to the south of KM 57
  This pond was colonized in the late 1990s.

- **The pond** at KM 72
  The beaver dam is an obvious structure right along the roadside.

Otters are regularly travel in family groups along creeks at all times of year.

River Otter

Because river otters frequent the same habitat as beavers, virtually any of the locations for that species could produce otters as well. Look at those sites in addition to the ones given below. Keep in mind that smaller creeks and larger lakes are travelled frequently by otters and that because they range widely, it is difficult to predict where they might appear at any given time.

Otter activity varies seasonally. Late fall and early spring, when the ice is retreating from the waterways, are usually the best times for finding these agile and playful animals. Here are some of my favourite viewing locations:

- **Forbes Creek,** at KM 40.1

- **The bridge** at KM 43.2
  Scan both up and downstream for otters.

- **The lake** at KM 44
  This a good potential spot for seeing otters.

- **Pretty Lake** at KM 54.5
  Otters regularly hunt along the shores of this lake.

MAP 8
EAST SIDE North from KM 24

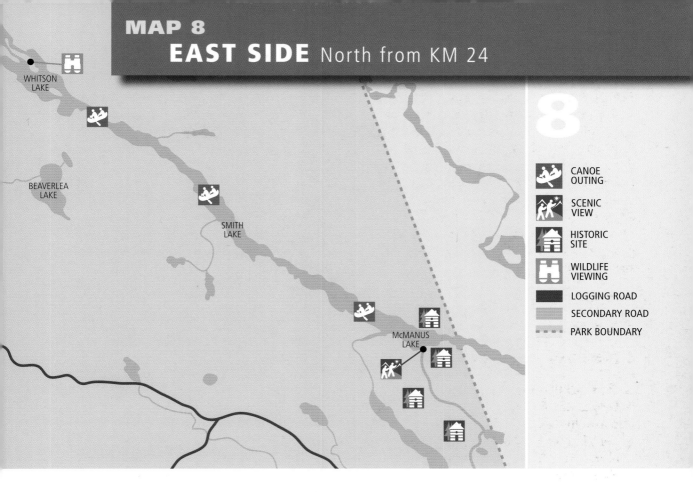

WHITSON LAKE

BEAVERLEA LAKE

SMITH LAKE

McMANUS LAKE

8

CANOE OUTING

SCENIC VIEW

HISTORIC SITE

WILDLIFE VIEWING

LOGGING ROAD

SECONDARY ROAD

PARK BOUNDARY

■ **Lake Travers marsh** 1.5 km (1mile) north from KM 69.4
Shortly after you reach the mill site, look for the marsh on your left. Also walk another short distance to the point and carefully scan Lake Travers for signs of these otters.

■ **Turtle Club Point, Lake Travers** KM 72
From the parking lot, walk east along the footpath that starts behind the bulletin board. This short route takes you to a point where the magnificent Turtle Club Lodge once stood. Only a few piles of rubble remain, along with the five stark chimneys that stand sentinel over the site of the buildings.

This point offers excellent views of the Petawawa River and the south end of Lake Travers. Otters hunt here for fish and crayfish year round. Early spring and late fall are the best seasons to look, as the strong current keeps the water open at the mouth of the river while the lake remains frozen. Otters use the edges of the ice as a dining table.

■ **KM 72**
You should also check the pond on the west side of the road at KM 72. Just beyond the KM 72 sign, the bridge over the Petawawa offers another vantage point. Downstream is the best direction to check, especially in winter.

BIRDS

As I did for the Highway 60 Corridor, I detail here the species most frequently sought by birders. In addition, I suggest a few locations for other species of interest.

Tips on locating particular species as well as attracting birds in general are given in the section "Observing Wildlife" (page 47).

Spruce Grouse

While spruce grouse are found in and near spruce bogs on the west side of Algonquin, on the East Side they are also seen in jack pine forests. This species is actually more common in this part of Algonquin and they are often observed, particularly at sunrise, picking grit from the Barron Canyon Road. Also, spruce grouse can be seen feeding in the jack pines bordering the road, especially in winter. If not visible from the road, they can be found by walking through the jack pines, especially in the following locations, which are typical spruce grouse habitats:

- **McManus Road** KM 24
  I have not seen a spruce grouse yet on this road, but this area looks very good for grouse. There is a wonderful black spruce bog to the right where you first take the road. Later, you drive through extensive jack pines as you approach McManus Lake.

- **Barron Canyon Road** from KM 61.5 to KM 62
  The black spruce/tamarack bog on the south side of the road is worth checking.

- **Barron Canyon Road** from KM 63 to 63.5
  The south side of the road, particularly the black spruce edge, is a regular spot.

- **Barron Canyon Road** from KM 65 to KM 70
  Spruce grouse are common through these jack pine flats. In particular, the pines near the Stuart Spur junction at KM 67 and along the stretch between KM 67.5 and KM 69.4 usually harbour grouse.

- **The Mill Site Road** north from KM 69.4
  I have frequently encountered spruce grouse by walking 1.5 km (1 mile) along the road that leads north to the abandonned mill site on Lake Travers.

Gray Jay

Gray jays are relatively common on this side of the Park but, unlike jays found along Highway 60, lack coloured bands on their legs, for research on this species is not conducted on the East Side. Regardless, these gentle birds will likely approach you for food, so be sure to have a chunk of bread or some other edible offering in hand when you encounter them.

A few of the regular places for gray jays are:

- **McManus Lake Road** KM 24
  This 8 km (5-mile) road frequently has gray jays at various locations.

- **Barron Canyon Trail** KM 28.9
  Gray jays are regularly seen along the trail but the parking lot remains one of the better places to see them.

- **Achray turn** KM 37.8
  Gray jays are frequently encountered at this junction.

- **Forbes Creek,** at KM 40.1
  This boreal stretch commonly produces gray jay sightings.

- **Pretty Lake** KM 54.5
  There is usually a family group of gray jays not far from the campsite.

- **The creek** in the vicinity of KM 62.2
  This a good place to look for this species.

- **Whitson Creek** KM 63.7
  One of the better spots for finding these and other northern birds.

- **The jack pine flats** KM 65–KM 72
  This area supports a number of gray jays.

- **The road to the mill site** (north from KM 69.4)
  The periphery of the open area, particularly near the marsh, usually has gray jays.

Black-backed woodpeckers, another "northern specialty" of the Park, are fairly common in East Side forests.

Black-backed Woodpecker

This northern woodpecker is relatively common on this side of Algonquin and I have seen them and heard them in the pines through most of this region, including along both interpretive trails and the Lake Travers Road.

Some of the more regular locations for this bird include:

- **McManus Road** KM 24
  One of the better spots on this generally good road is the black spruce bog that lies on the east (right) side of the road approximately 1 km (0.6 miles) north from the Lake Travers Road. However, you might encounter this species anywhere along this road.

- **KM 35.2**
  Check the dead trees along the creek.

- **KM 37**
  Look in the wet spruce/fir area.

- **Pretty Lake** KM 54.5

- **Barron Canyon Road** between KM 61.5 and KM 62.2

- **Whitson Creek** KM 63.7
  Although the area along the southeast side of the road is often productive, black-backed woodpeckers might be found anywhere in the vicinity of the creek.

- **Barron Canyon Road** from KM 65 to KM 72

- **KM 69.4**
  The road leading north, which is closed to vehicular traffic, is worth investigating.

OTHER SPECIES

Some species are more easily found on the East Side of Algonquin because of the extent of the pine/poplar forests. In particular, pine warblers, dark-eyed juncos and pileated woodpeckers are very common. A few additional species, including some of the East Side "specialties," are discussed below.

Red Crossbill

Because of the abundance of white pines, their preferred seed tree, red crossbills are usually present year round. In some years they occur in surprisingly large numbers and can be seen picking grit all along the Barron Canyon Road. In years of low numbers, two relatively reliable spots for encountering red crossbills are the Sand Lake gate and the Turtle Club site, just east of KM 72. At the latter location red crossbills are often found gleaning lime from the chimneys, particularly between late fall and spring.

Merlin

These agile falcons have increased dramatically in numbers in recent years and are now relatively common all through Algonquin, especially near East Side lakes. One pair usually nests close to Achray and occasionally chases swallows near the boat launch. These birds often utter rapidly repeated, high-pitched rising screams when they are nesting.

The Lake Travers area usually supports at least two pairs of merlins. They can often be seen either perching on the tops of dead snags or flying over the jack pine flats, especially between KM 63 and KM 71.5. One pair usually nests at the old mill site 1.5 km (1 mile) north of KM 69.4, and also hunts at the Turtle Club site (on the point east of the parking lot at KM 72).

Barred Owl

While perhaps not quite as common as they are along the Highway 60 Corridor, barred owls can be heard on the East Side at a number of locations.

- **Barron Canyon Trail** KM 28.9
  I have heard owls from the vicinity of the parking lot and from the top of the trail.

- **KM 37**
  This is one of the spots where I have traditionally heard barred owls at night, often just before the break of dawn.

- **Maple Forest on Achray Road** 1.2 km (0.7 mile) south from KM 37.8
  This mature stand of hardwoods, recently ravaged by logging, formerly had a dependable resident pair of barred owls.

Whip-poor-will and Common Nighthawk

Both of these birds are much more easily encountered on the East Side than along Highway 60. Nighthawks start hunting before dusk and are fairly easy to see. Their raspy *peent* calls and booming courtship sounds identify their whereabouts. Whip-poor-wills are also easy to hear due to their loud name-giving song, but are generally much tougher to see. However, they frequently sit on sandy roads and their eyes glow bright red in headlight beams. Thus, a slow drive in the right areas might produce a view of these tough-to-see birds.

Both species can be heard at Grand Lake and at numerous locations along the Barron Canyon Road, but the best area is in the jack pine flats between KM 64 and KM 67 (KM 66 is the optimal location). Try listening around dusk or just before sunrise.

MAP 9
EAST SIDE KM 28– KM 45

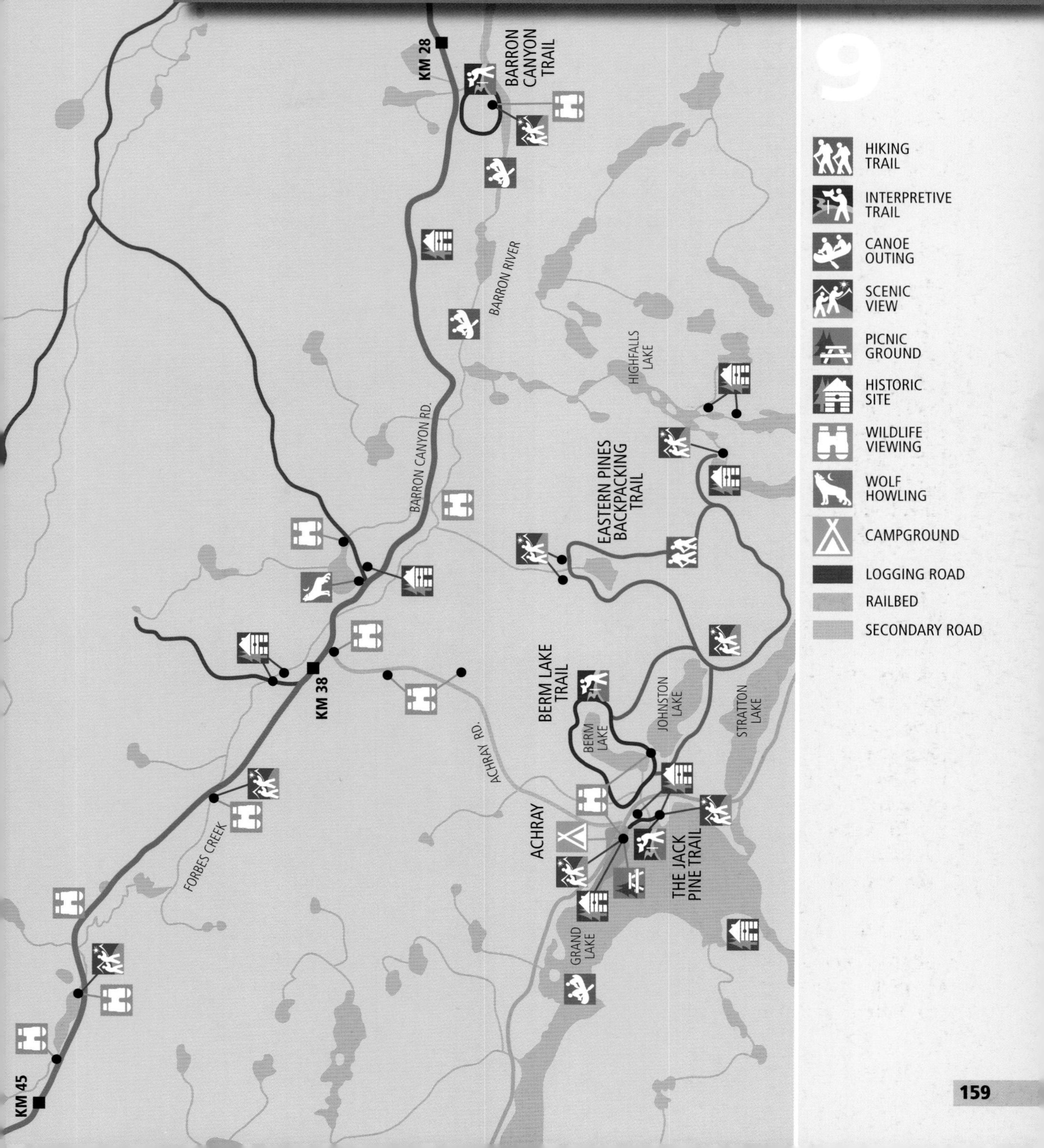

KM 28

BARRON CANYON TRAIL

BARRON RIVER

HIGHFALLS LAKE

BARRON CANYON RD.

EASTERN PINES BACKPACKING TRAIL

KM 38

ACHRAY RD.

BERM LAKE TRAIL

BERM LAKE

JOHNSTON LAKE

STRATTON LAKE

ACHRAY

THE JACK PINE TRAIL

GRAND LAKE

FORBES CREEK

KM 45

9

HIKING TRAIL

INTERPRETIVE TRAIL

CANOE OUTING

SCENIC VIEW

PICNIC GROUND

HISTORIC SITE

WILDLIFE VIEWING

WOLF HOWLING

CAMPGROUND

LOGGING ROAD

RAILBED

SECONDARY ROAD

OTHER HIGHLIGHTS

Because the topography and soils of the East Side are different from those of western Algonquin, some East Side flora and fauna are unique. Several phenomena in particular are noteworthy.

A healthy population of wood turtles, rare reptiles in North America, exists along the Petawawa River. These turtles are distinctive, possessing an ornate shell and orange front legs and throat. During the egg-laying season in early June, they are occasionally seen crossing Barron Canyon Road near Lake Travers. They are also found along the Petawawa River. If you are fortunate enough to come across a wood turtle, please do not disturb it.

Another turtle found on the East Side, one that is occasionally confused with the wood turtle, is the Blanding's turtle. This species, however, has a bright yellow throat and a smooth, highly domed, spotted shell.

In late May and early June in even-numbered years the Macoun's arctic, a boreal butterfly, flies in the larger jack pine stands near Lake Travers. It is pale orange and resembles a small washed-out monarch butterfly. Algonquin Park represents the southernmost range of this butterfly in Ontario.

Another noteworthy East Side phenomenon is the spectacular late-summer show of wildflowers along the rivers, particularly at Poplar Rapids on the Petawawa River (KM 72.1). From late July to mid-August the edges of the Petawawa (and in places, the Barron River) flame with the vibrant red blossoms of cardinal-flower. The small island just upstream from the bridge over Poplar Rapids annually exhibits one of the most exquisite wildflower gardens I have ever seen. Here, the soft pink of Joe-Pye weed, the yellow of grass-leaved goldenrod, the white of boneset and the crimson of cardinal-flower all blend to create a symphony of colour.

The wood turtle is an endangered species that is frequently encountered out of water.

POINTS OF HISTORICAL INTEREST

The East Side of Algonquin was one of the first to feel the logger's axe because of its rich supply of giant pines and its proximity to the Ottawa Valley, the hub of lumbering activity in eastern Ontario. The Petawawa River was extremely important in the transport of logs from the Park to the Ottawa River, and every spring swarms of men moved thousands of logs down its length. The last log drive in Algonquin Park took place on this river in 1959.

The rugged beauty of this side of Algonquin also attracted the attention of renowned artists. Tom Thomson not only sketched some of his most famous works on the East Side but he also worked here as a fire ranger in the summer of 1916. In addition to the sites related to logging and to Tom Thomson, the East Side has a number of other places of historical interest.

McManus Blowdown 6 km (3.7 miles) north from KM 24

On July 5, 1999, a severe windstorm known as a microburst touched down in the McManus Lake area. The winds snapped off pines and other trees as if they were matchsticks. The dramatic effects of the wind are still visible at several locations along the section of road between Frontier Lake and the boat launch on McManus Lake. The aftermath of the storm can also be seen on the far shore of McManus Lake directly across from the boat launch.

Other sites showing the effects of that wind include KM 50 (just west of the hydro line), KM 54.7 (west end of Pretty Lake), and the northwest corner of the mill site at Lake Travers (1.5 km/1 mile north of KM 69.4).

Logging Camp Remains KM 31.6

A boggy pond lies on the south side of the road. On the northwest side of this wetland you will find the remnants of a logging camp, which was built in the 1930s by a contractor for the Whitmore Lumber Company. An old well, foundations and assorted camp debris are still present. The ruins of an older camp, probably a camboose, are also located here.

Pine Forest Research Area KM 36.4

A research project on the dynamics of white pine growth was conducted here in 1929. A joint venture between the Department of Lands and Forests (now the Ministry of Natural Resources) and the University of Toronto, the study was the first of its kind in Ontario. Trees bearing numbered tags from this program can be found close to the junction of Barron Canyon Road and the logging road running north. The trees were measured again in 1949, but no further examination occurred until the 1980s.

CNR Rail Bed 5 km (3 miles south) of KM 37.8

As you enter Achray, you cross the abandoned Canadian National Railway line. This line was built through Algonquin between 1912 and 1915 by the Canadian Northern Railway. In 1918 Canadian Northern Railway was purchased by Canadian National Railway. The railway line ran under the latter name until 1995, when service was rerouted outside the Park onto the Canadian Pacific Railway line. The last train through this area of Algonquin was Train No. 114 on November 25, 1995. The steel rails and wooden ties were removed from the Park in 1996 and 1997. You can also access the rail bed at KM 67 (Stuart's Spur) and at KM 70.3 (see page 165).

10

ROWAN
LAKE

GRAND
LAKE

ARCAJOU
LAKE

ACHRAY

GRAND
LAKE

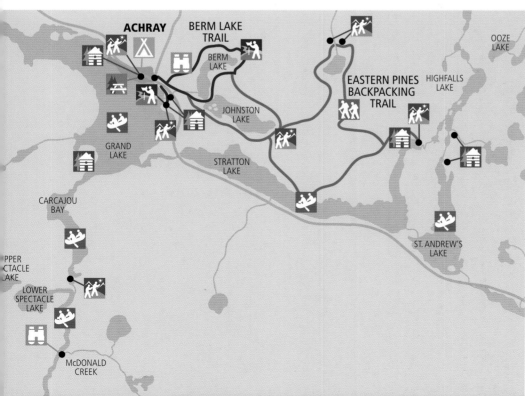

11

ACHRAY

BERM LAKE
TRAIL

BERM
LAKE

OOZE
LAKE

EASTERN PINES
BACKPACKING
TRAIL

HIGHFALLS
LAKE

JOHNSTON
LAKE

GRAND
LAKE

STRATTON
LAKE

CARCAJOU
BAY

ST. ANDREW'S
LAKE

PPER
CTACLE
LAKE

LOWER
SPECTACLE
LAKE

McDONALD
CREEK

	HIKING TRAIL
	INTERPRETIVE TRAIL
	CANOE OUTING
	SCENIC VIEW
	HISTORIC SITE
	WILDLIFE VIEWING
	WOLF HOWLING
	RAIL BED
	SECONDARY ROAD
	HYDRO LINE

Stone Building (Achray)

5 km (3 miles) south from KM 37.8

As you enter Achray, a large stone building lies directly ahead on Grand Lake. The building, erected in 1933 as an office for this part of Algonquin, was constructed of stone hauled from across the lake. It continues to be used as the headquarters for the East Side.

The Outside In Cabin (Achray)

This structure, used as a fire ranger's cabin in the early 1900s, is located just east of the stone building and is now an interpretive facility. Tom Thomson lived here in the summer of 1916 when he worked as a fire ranger. During his stay, he painted a sign bearing this unusual name (but spelled *Out-Side-In*). Unfortunately the original sign's whereabouts are currently unknown, but a replica is now posted on the cabin.

Tom Thomson, then an Algonquin fire-ranger, stayed in the Outside In, now an interpretive centre.

Site of Tom Thomson's *The Jack Pine* (Grand Lake)

Tom Thomson's famous painting was sketched in 1916 from a point just south of the Achray Campground. To reach this site, travel along the interpretive trail leading from the east end of the campground. The jack pine is gone, but the rolling hills across the lake easily identify this as the site of the famous work of art. An interpretive plaque stands at the site.

Ranke Sawmill Site and Log Chute north from KM 38.3

Walk up the road leading north from Barron Canyon Road. A short distance in, you will reach a gravel pit around which remnants of the Ranke Sawmill are still to be found. This mill was built, as many mills and logging camps were, on the site of a much older camp.

Just beyond the pit is Forbes Creek. Walk downstream a short distance to a small rapids. The flat planks along the creek are from the bottom of a log chute that once carried logs past these rapids.

Blowdown KM 50

The downed trees on both sides of the road are the result of 1999 windstorm that also created the McManus Blowdown.

Blowdown KM 54.7

More evidence of the same severe windstorm of can be seen just past the west end of Pretty Lake.

Stuart's Spur 0.5 km (0.3 mile) south from KM 67

Stuart was the manager of the Pembroke Shook Mills, which built a loading spur – a short section of rail – here in 1929. At this spur joining the now abandoned CNR line, pine logs were loaded onto flatcars by a steam hoist. On the high ground around the small parking area just north of Travers Creek once stood a number of buildings, including a stable, a blacksmith shop, a cookery and bunkhouses. The alder flats between the high ground and the now abandoned CNR Railway line formed the holding area for pine logs destined for the shook mills in Pembroke (shooks were prefab wooden boxes). A dam on Travers Creek kept the holding area flooded to prevent logs from becoming stained by exposure to the air before they were loaded for transport. The camp was in operation until 1954.

A more recent camp was run by Shaw Lumber on the opposite side of the rail bed in the vicinity of the large clearing. In order to transport the logs from this site, the railway spur was moved to that side of the former tracks. High quality red pine logs had their bark peeled before they were shipped for use as telephone, hydro or utility poles. Lower grade red pine and white pine logs were shipped directly to the Pembroke Shook Mills. This camp shut down in the late 1960s but was briefly opened for the 1980–81 season. In 1988 the camp was completely dismantled and the spur area replanted.

Pembroke Lumber Company Mill Site 1.5 km (1 mile) north from KM 69.4

Park safely off the main road and walk north on this "closed" road until you reach a large opening, the site of a mill run by the Pembroke Lumber Company. Built in the early 1930s, it ran until 1977, a phenomenal length of time for an isolated mill in Algonquin. Not much remains today except for debris scattered here and there. The most obvious remaining structure is a small water tower to your left as you approach the lake. The broken trees around the water tower are a result of the windstorm that took place on July 5, 1999.

CNR Railway Bed 1.3 km (0.8 mile) south from KM 70.3

Drive south on this road, keeping to the right when you reach the fork 0.8 km (0.5 miles) from the main road. After travelling another 0.5 km (0.3 mile), you reach the rail bed. Several small buildings, including a small station house, formerly stood on the far side of the rail bed, to the right of the pond, which is currently occupied by beavers. The buildings were taken down shortly after the railway line was removed.

Radio Observatory KM 70.3 and KM 71.5

This area was set aside in 1959 for the National Research Council (NRC) and was returned to provincial jurisdiction in 1996. While much of the original operation has been shut down, a large radio telescope, known as the "Big Dish," is still used to search for radio signals from outer space. The Big Dish is on the private road leading west from KM 71.5, but it can sometimes be partially seen by looking west past the pond at KM 72. An inactive bank of smaller dishes, used for solar observation, formerly stood along the road south from KM 70.3.

The research complex, last staffed by the NRC in the late 1980s, was operated for a number of ensuing years by the Institute for Space and Terrestrial Science (ISTS). From 1991 to 1993, ISTS also held a Space Camp at this site. At the time of writing, the complex is operated by Natural Resources Canada (NRCan).

Turtle Club Site east from KM 72

Park in the lot for water access to Lake Travers and look for the footpath that starts from behind the information board. The path leads a short distance to the point where the Turtle Club was situated. Built in 1933, this was a private lodge owned by the family of the famous lumber entrepreneur J.R. Booth. Five chimneys plus a pile of debris mark the site where the unique structure formerly stood. The elegant log building was constructed in the shape of a turtle, Booth's bark mark (a mark inscribed, usually by axe, on the side of logs to identify the owner). The building was purchased by the government in 1973 and was dismantled five years later.

Glance Piers KM 72.1

If you stand on the bridge over Poplar Rapids and look upstream, you will see piers of piled rocks jutting into the Petawawa River. Probably built well before the turn of the previous century, these rock piles kept logs away from the shoreline and directed them into the channel during spring river drives. For more than 100 years, the Petawawa River carried logs from Algonquin Park to the Ottawa River. The last log drive in the Park took place on this river in 1959.

Although the vegetation has filled out since this photo was taken, the Turtle Club chimneys are still standing.

MAP 12
EAST SIDE KM 42–KM 64

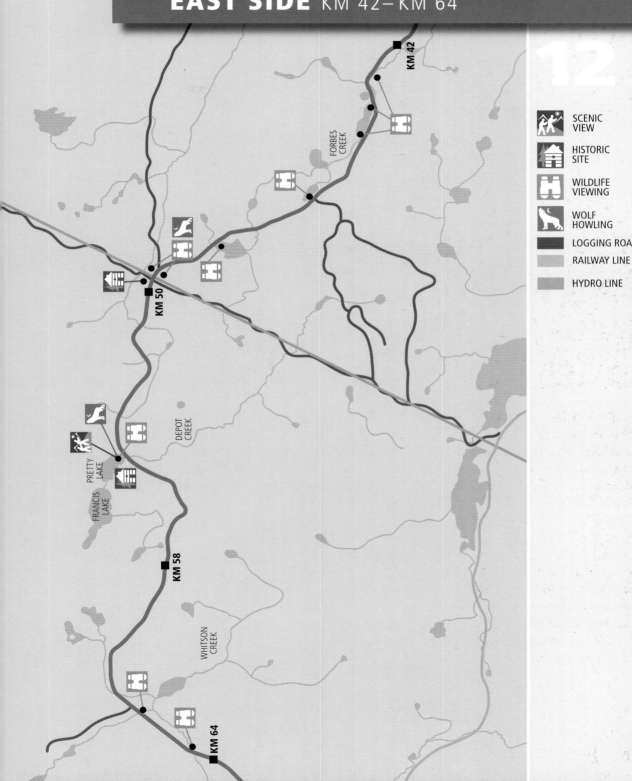

12

SCENIC VIEW

HISTORIC SITE

WILDLIFE VIEWING

WOLF HOWLING

LOGGING ROAD

RAILWAY LINE

HYDRO LINE

KM 42

FORBES CREEK

KM 50

DEPOT CREEK

PRETTY LAKE

FRANCIS LAKE

KM 58

WHITSON CREEK

KM 64

CANOEING IN THE EAST SIDE

Although fewer in number, many of the canoe routes on the East Side are more dramatic than those in the Highway Corridor. Another major difference is that fabulous whitewater canoeing is available for those who seek it. The Petawawa River is renowned for this feature, but only people with considerable experience should attempt to "shoot" the rapids. For canoeing this river I highly recommend the *Petawawa River Whitewater Guide*, produced by the Friends of Algonquin Park. The map-brochure *Canoe Routes of Algonquin Provincial Park* shows the campsites, the location of the rapids and the portages that bypass them, but does not go into the detail that the *Petawawa River Whitewater Guide* offers.

AVAILABLE SERVICES

There are no rental services on the East Side. However, the Algonquin Portage Store, which is 21 km (13 miles) before the Sand Lake gate, offers complete outfitting and shuttle services. At time of writing, Achray Campground has a few canoes and kayaks for rent to people using that facility.

Still relatively unexplored, Algonquin's East Side offers many excellent day outings for canoe or kayak.

RECOMMENDED SHORT TRIPS

The following are all short excursions, one day or less, that could be extended into longer trips if desired. Remember, cans and bottles are prohibited in the Interior and camping permits are required for overnight stays. The map-brochure *Canoe Routes of Algonquin Provincial Park* is essential for any canoe trip in the Park.

Barron River

The 100 metre (330-foot) cliffs of Barron Canyon make canoeing the Barron River an awe-inspiring event. The river can be reached from Squirrel Rapids (KM 20.3) or from the Brigham Lake access (KM 33.2). Both sites have parking facilities. The Brigham Lake access is closer to the canyon but has a steeper access to the water.

From Squirrel Rapids to the canyon you are paddling against a gentle current, but the return trip, obviously, is easier. One enjoyable way of doing this route is to travel in two parties. One vehicle can be dropped off at Squirrel Rapids, making the trip a one-way excursion from the Brigham Lake Access. Note that there are four portages on the route (the longest 440 m/480 yards), three upstream and one downstream of the canyon.

When you journey through the canyon, you are travelling back in time. Birds that usually nest on man-made structures can be seen nesting on these cliffs as they have done for thousands of years. As you paddle along the sheer wall of rock, watch for the mud nests of barn swallows cemented under overhangs at about eye level. Flowing streams of dried excrement below the nests identify their location. As you approach active nests, the adult birds noisily dive-bomb your canoe. Eastern phoebes, less aggressive birds, share the same recesses, but their nests are coated with moss and lichen.

Higher up on the cliff faces, the bulky stick nests of common ravens can also be seen. From the tops of the cliffs, red-tailed hawks indignantly screech in protest at your intrusion into their domain.

The cliff faces are also home to a variety of intriguing plants. Some are species from the far north that remain as tokens of the cold past. Others thrive here because of the lime that percolates from rock crevices. Because lime is rare in Algonquin, a number of the plants you paddle alongside are unique to the canyon. The lichen xanthoria, a northern lime-lover, is responsible for the beautiful orange that coats much of the exposed rock. Another plant to look for is the encrusted saxifrage, made easily identifiable by the white dots of lime it exudes around the periphery of its leaves, which grow in a basal rosette.

The roar of the river is now silenced, as is the thunder of log drives that occurred here in more recent times. The Barron River was an important route for spring drives, and millions of logs passed through here from the mid-1800s to the early 1900s. The grave of one unfortunate driver lies along the river at the second campsite below the canyon, hidden by a clump of conifers.

Along the river you will find old logs left behind from these drives. Check the ends carefully for the timber stamp of J.R. Booth, the renowned lumber baron. The stamp was a diamond with the initials "JB" inside it. Time has likely erased the marks but they were visible in the not-so-distant past.

The indistinct ruins of a log chute can be found at Cache Rapids, the first set of rapids upstream from Squirrel Rapids.

Grand Lake

Despite the presence of motorboats (up to 10-horsepower motors are allowed), Grand Lake is a marvellous body of water to paddle. Several options exist as to where you can go and what you can see on a day's paddle from Achray, 5 km (3 miles) south from KM 37.8.

Option 1: Grand Lake

A full day can be spent paddling to the lake's northwest extremity and back. I would allow a minimum of eight hours for this, so it's best to start at dawn to give plenty of time for exploring.

With its narrow configuration, Grand Lake is more like a river than a lake. Two points of interest lie along this route. Approximately halfway up the lake, on the west side, is the portage to Wenda Lake. Discarded mechanical items and an old root cellar, which identify the site of a former lumber camp, can be found near the start of the portage.

The remains of the McLachlin Depot, a central supply settlement for lumbering operations in the area, are located at the north end of the large bay at the northeast corner of Grand Lake. At one time logs were hauled overland on wooden rails by a steam locomotive with double-flange wheels, and then deposited in Grand Lake.

One of the few cattail marshes in Algonquin sits at the very top end of the lake. Here great blue herons and American bitterns stalk frogs along the narrow creek that meanders through the marsh. If you are fortunate, you might startle a Virginia rail into uttering its alarm call, a weird *wugh-wugh-wugh-wugh-wugh* that sounds like a giant coin wobbling to a halt after being spun on a tabletop. These secretive birds also emit a sharp *dik-dik-kidik-kidik*. The Grand Lake marsh supports the highest density of Virginia rails in the Park. Beavers and moose visit the marsh to feast on the dense growth of water-shield and water-lilies that grow where it meets the lake. Wolves also visit the area in search of these large prey.

Across the logging road at the north end of the marsh lies Clemow Lake, the beautiful body of water depicted in the coniferous forest diorama in the Algonquin Visitor Centre. A lumber camp formerly stood at the north end of this lake at the site of the northernmost campsite.

Option 2: Carcajou Bay

Carcajou is a French word that means "wolverine." Although these large weasels are not currently known in the Park, the use of this word in naming a bay, a lake and a creek has given rise to the suggestion that at one time wolverines may have been present here. It is, however, most unlikely that this northern weasel was found this far south, apart from the period just after glaciation.

The route is a beautiful one but it should be done well after black fly season ends. The East Side is notoriously bad for these insects during the month of June, and the Carcajou area seems to host the highest population in the world!

After you leave Achray, a relatively short paddle brings you across the lake. Before entering the bay you pass by an island with a herring gull colony. At times the gulls have an intriguing method of nest defence – they fly over your canoe and either vomit rotting fish or defecate. Thus, I suggest you give the island a wide berth.

Once in the "safety" of the bay, carefully check the rocks on your right (the north side). Indian pictographs – quite faded but still discernible – pass on their ancient message from just above eye level on the low cliffs immediately after you enter the bay. I have found that splashing water on the symbols enhances their colour.

The dramatic rocky hills bordering Carcajou Bay make this a particularly enjoyable route. It is these hills from the bay region that form the backdrop for Tom Thomson's *The Jack Pine*, painted from the Achray side. A delightful little waterfall tumbles into the south end of the bay. After one short portage, you have the choice of taking another short portage and canoeing into Lower Spectacle Lake or continuing up McDonald Creek, a winding bog-lined waterway and an excellent moose-viewing area in summer.

Option 3: Stratton Lake

After leaving Achray, paddle along the south shore of the lake, past the extensive sand beaches where early Algonkians once camped. Soon after entering the narrows you will reach a short portage skirting the dam. Stratton Lake lies on the far side of the portage. It is a beautiful rock-bound body of water that seems more like a narrow river than an actual lake. Ospreys and river otters are frequently seen as they search for fish in the clear waters. Since this was an important waterway for log drives in earlier years, evidence of that activity still abounds.

Once at the south end of the lake, you have the choice of taking a portage (45 m/50 yards) into St. Andrew's Lake or paddling to the end of the bay that runs north from here. I would suggest you do both – but obviously not at the same time! High Falls thunders down from the end of the north-running bay, and the remains of a logging camp on the extreme northern tip are a legacy of the lake's history.

St. Andrew's Lake harbours a couple of fascinating relics from early logging days. A pointer boat, a logging vessel narrowed at both ends, rests at the bottom of the lake at its northern extremity, just before the portage and closer to the far shore. If the water surface is not ruffled by wind, you should be able to see it by peering into the water.

Another bit of history lies along the portage into Highfalls Lake. The remnants of the wooden log chute used to shepherd logs around the rapids beside the portage are still apparent. The best section stretches between the pond approximately halfway along the portage and the end of the portage at Highfalls Lake.

Because the chute is on the far side of the rapids, which the portage parallels, you may be interested in walking along that side to view it. After you finish the portage to Highfalls Lake, you can paddle to the opposite shore and walk back up the rapids.

From here, if time permits, you can travel on to Barron Canyon, but you must carry your canoe or kayak across several small portages to reach it. If two parties are involved, one vehicle could be left at Squirrel Rapids access so that you paddle downstream through the Barron Canyon and do not have to retrace your steps (or "strokes"!). If you do a one-way trip, be sure to start early in the day to avoid paddling in the dark.

The ruins of an early logging camp can be seen along the portage between Opalescent and Ooze lakes, and the remains of a cabin, possibly a river drivers' shelter, lie halfway along the portage (285 m/310 yards) between Ooze Lake and the Cascades.

Lake Travers

This lake, one of my favourites in all of Algonquin, offers excellent canoeing. However, on windy days Lake Travers can be rough, so keep abreast of the weather situation while you're on it.

From the parking lot and boat launch at KM 72, you can put your canoe directly into the Petawawa River. As you paddle along, you are following the route of the early river drivers. The point on your right bearing tall chimneys is the site of the Turtle Club, described in "Points of Historical Interest" (page 166).

If you paddle east around the south edge of the lake, you will pass below a few buildings associated with the Radio Observatory complex. Beyond these lies an interesting marsh that is full of life, particularly at daybreak. I have seen great blue herons, American bitterns, white-tailed deer, raccoons, moose, muskrat, river otters and beavers in this terrific marsh, as well as rare visitors such as a black-crowned night heron, a great egret and a snowy egret.

From here you paddle north past the old mill site, with the remnants of a dock and other buildings visible along the rocky point. Beyond it, there lies a shallow bay with a long sand beach. Farther north, the scenery becomes more dramatic as steep hills embrace the lake where it narrows back into a river.

The large island just before the narrows is a moose-calving spot in mid-May. On occasion, it harbours nesting merlins. A point bearing an old logging camp lies about 0.5 km (0.3 mile) beyond the small island and the campsites in the narrows. The site is on the west side of the river and is hidden by alders. About another 3 km (2 miles) past this you will see that most of the trees on the hillside to the right of you have been knocked down. This blowdown occurred during a windstorm in 1983. Just beyond that spot lies the portage around Big Thomson Rapids. Remnants of a wooden logging dam are quite evident near the start of the portage. Unless you plan to continue down the Petawawa on an overnight excursion, this portage will be the place where you turn back.

McManus, Smith and Whitson Lakes

These so-called lakes are simply widenings of the Petawawa River. To access McManus Lake, take the well-marked road at KM 24. The parking lot and water access are 8 km (5 miles) from the turn.

On the first leg of this trip you paddle against a gentle current. There are only two small portages along the route, the first a mere 90 m (100 yards) long. If the water is high enough and you have the strength, it is possible to bypass this portage by paddling up the rapids, but believe me, this is tough work and the portage is a considerably easier option.

While these lakes offer pleasant canoeing, the landscape is less varied than along the other routes. This route does, however, have some interesting tree species growing along its shores. One finds the southern silver maple and the northern green alder, the latter a rare shrub in the Park. Green alder has sticky young leaves and branchlets, and the cone-like catkins are held on long stalks. Speckled alder, its abundant relative, has dry leaves and branchlets, and short-stalked catkins.

On the small islands in Whitson Lake, silver maples are prolific. These southern trees are rare in most of Algonquin but not along the Petawawa River. The leaves of this maple are very deeply cut in contrast to those of its relatives. The rising song of warbling vireos, a southern species rare elsewhere in the Park, can sometimes be heard from the islands.

The return trip is virtually effortless since you will now be travelling with the current all the way back to your starting point.

MAP 13
EAST SIDE KM 64– KM 72

13

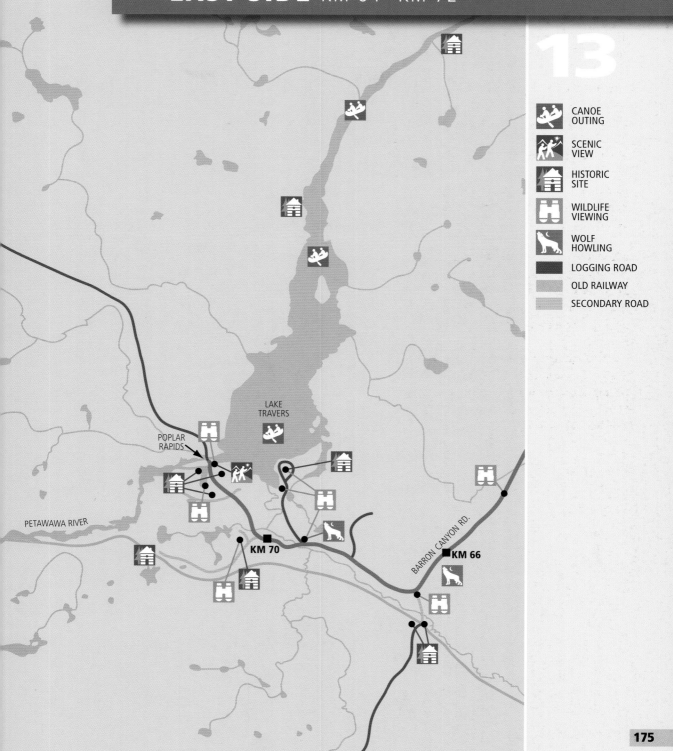

CANOE OUTING

SCENIC VIEW

HISTORIC SITE

WILDLIFE VIEWING

WOLF HOWLING

LOGGING ROAD

OLD RAILWAY

SECONDARY ROAD

LAKE TRAVERS

POPLAR RAPIDS

PETAWAWA RIVER

KM 70

BARRON CANYON RD.

KM 66

BASIN DEPOT

This south-east section of Algonquin remains one of the least used, which is rather surprising because it possesses a wealth of animal life, fascinating historic sites, several walking trails and its own special beauty, including a spectacular waterfall. For the camper, several drive-in Interior campsites on water are available, most of them all through summer and fall. As an alternative to these campsites, Bonnechere Provincial Park, a mere 15 minutes by car from the Algonquin boundary, offers camping with full services. Bonnechere Provincial Park is not only just a stone's-throw away but it offers a number of special programs in the Basin Depot area of Algonquin. Annual Public Wolf Howls and an archaeology program are current examples.

The Basin Depot area has a long history of logging and sparse settlement. Logging began in the Bonnechere Valley before 1830. The Bonnechere River, which the Basin Road roughly parallels, was formerly used for log transport during spring drives. In the summer months this meandering waterway becomes more of a creek and, for much of its length, is not traversable by canoe. Basin Depot, a supply depot and stopover spot for lumbermen, was the centre of logging activity between the mid-1800s and 1913. One

High Falls on the Bonnechere River is well worth a visit in early spring.

of the buildings, repaired in recent years by the Algonquin Forestry Authority, is the oldest building still standing in Algonquin.

Basin Road is an unpaved road that stretches 26 km (16 miles) from the Park boundary to the end of public access at the hydro line. There are three short side branches that you can take by vehicle (if road conditions allow). Two lead to Basin and Foys lakes, and the third, to a beautiful section of the Bonnechere River.

Although there are no facilities along this road, the area is well worth visiting for its wildlife, history, scenery and notable lack of people! Every kilometre of the Basin Road is marked with a KM sign, as is the case along the Highway 60 Corridor and the Barron Canyon Road.

The marking system for the Basin Road begins at the intersection of Turner's Road and the Paugh Lake Road, which leads south 200 metres (220 yards) past the end of the pavement. The Park boundary is 8.5 km (5.3 miles) west of this point, halfway between the KM 8 and KM 9 markers, and thus will de designated as KM 8.5.

Basin Depot is situated at KM 14.2. At KM 21.9 a wonderful coldwater spring has been routed into a dispensing pipe on the south side of the road.

Access to this part of Algonquin is achieved by travelling west on Turner's Road from County Road 58, just north of the entrance into Bonnechere Provincial Park. Turner's Road is approximately 40 km (25 miles) west of Pembroke.

The Basin Depot region supports pine and poplar forests that are representative of the entire northeastern two thirds of the Park. In addition, jack pines are prevalent in some areas, particularly just past the Park boundary and just before the hydro line. These pines harbour Canada's southernmost population of Macoun's arctic, a northern butterfly that, interestingly, appears in the adult form only on even-numbered years.

The Basin Road forests and ponds are habitat for a variety of wildlife including moose, beavers and a large population of white-tailed deer. In turn, these animals support several packs of eastern wolves, which can readily be heard at the appropriate times of year. Bonnechere Provincial Park, an excellent park to camp in while visiting the Basin region, offers a Public Wolf Howl, led by yours truly, on the third (or rarely fourth) Saturday of every August. Details can be found on the Bonnechere Park website: www.bonnecherepark.on.ca.

There are no campgrounds in the Basin Depot region of Algonquin, but there are a number of drive-in Interior campsites. Four of these are situated on Basin Lake (1.5 km/1 mile north of KM 14.2), three at Foys Lake (4 km/2.5 miles north of KM 23.6), two on the Bonnechere River (1.2 km/0.7 miles south of KM 30.6), one on Little Norway Lake (KM 31.1) and one at the hydro line where it meets the Bonnechere River (KM 34.3). These sites can be reserved through Provincial Park Reservations (1-800-ONT-PARK) or through Bonnechere Provincial Park (613-757-2672), and they are also available without reservations on a first-come, first-served basis. Be aware that the rules for Interior camping, such as no cans or bottles, apply to these sites.

Day-use and Interior camping permits for the Basin Depot region of Algonquin can be purchased at the Bonnechere Provincial Park office, just south of where Turner's Road leaves County Road 58, 15 km (9 miles) southeast of the Algonquin park boundary.

The Basin Road twists its way through a younger mixed forest for much of its length.

WALKING TRAILS

While there are no self-guiding Interpretive Trails in this part of Algonquin, there are a number of lovely walking trails that take you to scenic and historic sites. The trailhead of each one is usually marked with a sign bearing a pinecone symbol. The small booklet *Walks of the Little Bonnechere River* (by Roderick MacKay and Mark Stabb) shows the location and offers a brief overview of the human and natural history highlights of each trail. This inexpensive booklet is available at the Bonnechere Park office and bookstore, and at the Algonquin Visitor Centre bookstore.

Two of the trails detailed in *Walks of the Little Bonnechere River* lie either partly or fully outside Algonquin, but are well worth taking:

The McDonald grave stands as a stark reminder of the difficulties faced by the Park's first settlers.

■ **Whispering Winds Lookout on Egg Rock** KM 8
This trail, which begins just before the Algonquin boundary, climbs to a hilltop that offers a magnificent view of the Bonnechere Valley.

■ **Payne's Pine Trail** KM 8.9
This trail, which starts across from Argue Lake in Algonquin Park, quickly meanders across the park boundary to the shore of Stringer's Lake. After it leaves the lake, the trail travels along the top of a great sand bluff overlooking the Bonnechere River. Here, mats of bearberry sprawl across the sand slope, and silver maples, rare in Algonquin, abound in the floodplain of the river down below.

The rest of the trails detailed here are fully located in Algonquin.

■ **Sligo** KM 11.2
The Sligo trail, which starts across the road from a babbling section of the Bonnechere River, visits the site of a former hotel and farm. A white cross marks the 1883 burial site of Alexander McDonald, infant son of Ronald and Catherine McDonald, who farmed here until they were forced to leave, as were all "squatters."

■ **Basin Depot** KM 14.2
The Basin Depot trail takes you through the site of what was a busy settlement more than a hundred years ago. Highlights include Basin Cabin, the oldest building in Algonquin Park, and the gravesites of former residents of the Depot.

- **High Falls** KM 16.3
The High Falls trail brings you to a spectacular waterfall that roars its mightiest in early spring. It alone makes the two-hour roundtrip more than worthwhile. As you travel along the old tote road (a road used for hauling supplies by horse and wagon to loggers and homesteaders) that makes up most of the trail, watch at eye-level for vertical scars on red maple trunks. These were caused by moose tearing off strips of the bark in early spring.

- **McGuey Farm** KM 24.3
The clearing along the Bonnechere River that this trail leads to marks the former homestead of Dennis and Margaret McGuey. The open area is now a foraging place for mammals, including moose and white-tailed deer. Eastern wolves have denned here and have used the grassy meadow for rendezvous sites. A side trail leading north brings you to a small lake and the site of Bridge Dam.

- **McIntyre's Clearing** KM 33.5
When you reach the hydro line, look for a gated road leading off to the right. The trail starts here and after a short distance brings you to a large clearing on the left that remains somewhat a mystery. To reach the clearing, once you start descending the large hill past the gate on the logging road, look for a side trail beside a large red pine. The clearing will be visible through the trees. In his research for *Spirits of the Little Bonnechere*, historian Roderick MacKay learned of a legendary village that may well have stood at this site, which offers a grand view of the Bonnechere River. Eastern wolves regularly use this opening as a rendezvous site in late summer and fall.

WILDLIFE-VIEWING AREAS

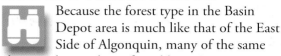 Because the forest type in the Basin Depot area is much like that of the East Side of Algonquin, many of the same plants and animals are found here. Porcupines are present thanks to the prevalence of trembling aspen. The road passes by several ponds and other small waterways that present opportunities to view animals such as river otters, moose and beavers. See "Observing Wildlife" (page 47) for suggestions on how to find these and other animals.

Moose
Although they might be encountered anywhere along the road, moose are seen more regularly in early summer when feeding on the sodium-rich aquatic plants in waterways along the road. A few of the better locations are given here.

- **Argue Lake** KM 8.8

- **Pond** at KM 19.5

- **Pond** at KM 27.6
Traditionally a "hot spot" for moose.

- **Wetland** at KM 30.8

- **Pond and creek** at KM 31.1

- **Bonnechere River** KM 32.2

- **Bonnechere River** at the hydro line (KM 34.3)
An area just upstream on the river beyond the gate marking the end of public access can be good in summer, and the hydro line area is also worth checking for moose during the rut. However, be aware that Native hunting does take place in this part of Algonquin in the fall.

The open space along the hydro line often offers views of moose, white-tailed deer, black bears or even eastern wolves.

White-tailed Deer

Since the entire area is good for seeing deer, it's possible to encounter them anywhere along the road. The large openings around Basin Depot (KM 14.2) are often productive.

Black Bear

Black bears, which also might be encountered anywhere along the main road, often forage for berries along the hydro line at the end of the Basin Road (KM 34). Dawn and late evening are the best times for looking there.

Eastern Wolf

The Basin Road road transects one of the better areas for wolf activity because of the abundance of white-tailed deer and beaver, wolves' principal prey. Whenever you discover fresh signs (i.e., tracks or scat) along the road, try some howling attempts (see "Observing Wildlife," page 47).

It's possible to come across wolves anywhere along the Basin Road but a few of the better locations for hearing and potentially seeing them are:

- Park Boundary KM 8.5
  This is an excellent spot for howling because you are on a rise of land adjacent to the Bonnechere Valley. Sound carries extremely well here and the valley throws back echoes that enhance your experience. From this spot I have heard wolves answer on many occasions, including Bonnechere Public Wolf Howls.

- Basin Depot KM 14.2

- Foys Lake turn KM 23.6

- Bonnechere River 1.2 km (0.7 mile) south of KM 30.6

- Little Norway Lake KM 31.1

- Bonnechere River KM 32.2

- Hydro Line KM 33.5

Beaver

Beavers are quite common along this road, as they are in the Bonnechere River you drive along before you reach the Algonquin boundary. At the time of writing, the following locations were occupied by beavers:

- **Stringer's Lake** KM 18.5
  Beaver lodges and their makers can be viewed by looking out across the boggy end of the lake from the Park boundary, albeit at some distance from you. Occasionally, beavers occupy the small pond on your right at the base of the hill you climbed to get to this location.

- **Argue Lake** KM 8.8
  This has been one of my favourite locations for observing and photographing beavers. They often feed and groom on the bog mats very close to the Basin Road. My experience has been that the crack of dawn is the best time to see beavers in this pond.

- **Pond** at KM 10.1

- **Pond** at KM 19.5

- **The pond** 1.0 km (0.6 mile) north from KM 23.6 (Foys Lake turn)

- **The pond** at KM 22.6
  This area was colonized by beavers in 2007.

- **Creek** at KM 24.4

- **Pond** at KM 26

- **Pond** at KM 27.6

- **Pond** at KM 29.6

- **Wetland** at KM 30.8

- **Little Norway Lake** KM 31.1

- **Bonnechere River** KM 32.2
  If you scan the river here you may not spot a beaver, but several lodges are visible along the water's edge.

River Otter
Because River Otters travel far and wide, their whereabouts are not as predictable as those of beavers. However, they are frequently seen in ponds and creeks along the Basin Road, especially Argue Lake (KM 8.8), and any of the locations suggested for beaver and moose might produce otters. In addition, the creek along the north side of the road from KM 20.8 to KM 21 is particularly good for otter activity.

BIRDS
The pine and poplar forests of the Basin Depot area support a bird fauna similar to that found on the East Side. Gray jays are generally easily viewed along the Basin Road, as are black-backed woodpeckers. Pileated woodpeckers are also quite common, and red crossbills and evening grosbeaks are regularly encountered.

Gray Jay and Black-backed Woodpecker
Due to the prevalence of northern coniferous forests bordering wetlands along the Basin Road, both these northern species are commonly encountered. A few locations that might offer better opportunities for seeing one or both species are:

- **Park Boundary** KM 8.5

- **Argue Lake** KM 8.8

- **Basin Depot** KM 14.2

- **Roadside** at KM 21.6

- **Roadside** from KM 24 to KM 26

- **Roadside** from KM 30.8 to KM 31.1

- **Bonnechere River** KM 32.2

- **Bonnechere River** KM 33.8

POINTS OF HISTORICAL INTEREST

Because of early settlement and the area's importance to the logging industry, Basin Road is richly endowed with historic sites. When Algonquin Park was expanded to include this area in 1914, the earliest settlers were deemed "squatters." Since they didn't hold formal title, their land was taken over and the families were ousted. For an excellent discussion of the early history of the Bonnechere River and the Basin Depot area, I highly recommend *Spirits of the Little Bonnechere* by Roderick MacKay.

The recently created walking trails bring you to many of these sites. The booklet *Walks of the Little Bonnechere River* (also co-authored by MacKay), which is available at Bonnechere Provincial Park and the Algonquin Visitor Centre bookstore, discusses more of the local history.

Basin Road KM 8.5 to KM 14.4

The present road generally follows the original Basin Road that ran from Eganville to Basin Depot (situated just beyond KM 14). Built in the mid-1800s, the Basin Road was an important supply route to the depot that serviced all the logging operations in this area.

In 1967 Martin Garvey, a homesteader's son raised only a few kilometres past the boundary, recollected that in 1909 this road had been incredibly busy with supplies for the lumbering operations. Each day, between 4 p.m. and sunset, as many as 40 teams of horses pulling supply wagons passed along the road. Over the entire day many more teams travelled the road.

McDonald Grave – Sligo KM 11.2

This grave is marked by a white cross and picket fence. James McDonald cleared this area for farming sometime in the mid- to late 1800s. Alexander McDonald, the infant son of Ronald,

a brother of James, was buried here in 1888. The inscription on the cross is still clearly legible. The McDonalds lived on this farm until the government took it over in 1914.

This area was once known as "Sligo" after the place in Ireland where Paddy Garvey, another early settler, was born. Sometime after 1855, Garvey set up Sligo House, a stopping place for lumbermen, just south of here along the Bonnechere. After 1870 Garvey concentrated on farming at the following site.

Garvey's Homestead KM 12.5

Paddy Garvey, who ran Sligo House, farmed here from about 1870 to 1914. As was the case with other "squatters" like the McDonald family, he was uprooted when the Park's boundaries were expanded in 1914.

Basin Depot KM 14.2 to KM 14.4

This open area with two (currently) standing buildings has a long and interesting history. This site was important as a central supply and stopover place for lumbermen because it was situated at the junction of two main supply routes. One of them ran north from Basin Creek to Grand Lake. The other ran parallel to the Bonnechere River to a depot at White Partridge Lake, and then continued through to Radiant Lake.

While the exact date of the first building is unknown, in 1843 four shanties were present. By 1890 there were 10 buildings, including a blacksmith shop, a post office and the Basin House, a large building containing a men's bar and living quarters. Between 1949 and 1960 the depot was run by Shoosplin Woods Limited. During this time 18 buildings stood here and the depot employed 98 men. A ranger cabin, built around the turn of the previous century, was removed from this site in the 1970s.

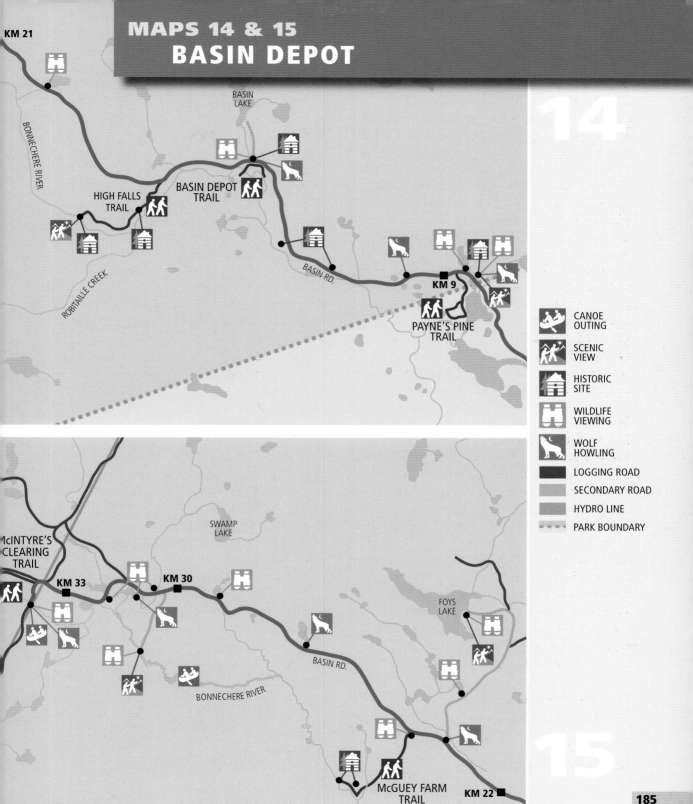

14

KM 21

BASIN LAKE

BONNECHERE RIVER

HIGH FALLS TRAIL

BASIN DEPOT TRAIL

ROBITAILLE CREEK

BASIN RD.

KM 9

PAYNE'S PINE TRAIL

CANOE OUTING

SCENIC VIEW

HISTORIC SITE

WILDLIFE VIEWING

WOLF HOWLING

LOGGING ROAD

SECONDARY ROAD

HYDRO LINE

PARK BOUNDARY

McINTYRE'S CLEARING TRAIL

SWAMP LAKE

KM 33

KM 30

FOYS LAKE

BONNECHERE RIVER

BASIN RD.

McGUEY FARM TRAIL

KM 22

15

The small log building at KM 14.2 was constructed in 1892 by the McLachlin Lumber Company. Originally built as an office, it served as a hospital during a diphtheria epidemic that same year. In 1909 it functioned again as an office for the John D. McRae Lumber Company. After the ownership had transferred at least twice more, the building was used as a school from 1911 to 1913. The cabin has also served as a harness shop and a summer residence, and is the oldest building still standing in Algonquin Park.

Along the east bank of Basin Creek on either side of the Basin Road lie two graves enclosed in white picket fences. It is believed that these are either graves of rivermen who drowned during an 1895 spring log drive along the Bonnechere or graves of victims of the 1892 diphtheria outbreak.

On the west side of Basin Creek is a large decrepit building that was apparently built by the McLachlin Lumber Company. After 1940 it served as a warehouse and storage facility for the Department of Lands and Forests (now the Ministry of Natural Resources). In recent years the building has begun to collapse and it may well be levelled by the time you visit Basin Depot. The poplar grove behind this building reportedly contains graves of victims of the 1892 diphtheria epidemic.

If you walk to the end of the open area on the south side of the Basin Road directly across from the road to Basin Lake, you will eventually come to a very pretty spot on the Bonnechere River just below where Basin Creek flows into it. In the fringe of trees bordering the river, look for the leaves and, if early enough in the year, for the unusual blooms of the nodding trillium, an uncommon flower, which grows here.

McGuey Farm KM 24.3
See "Walking Trails," page 181.

McIntyre's Clearing KM 33.5
See "Walking Trails," page 181.

CANOEING IN THE BASIN DEPOT AREA

 The Bonnechere River is not well endowed with canoe routes, for along much of its course it is a meandering, marshy waterway, more creek-like than river-like, with numerous beaver dams across it. However, it is rich in life, and great blue herons, American black ducks, moose, beaver and river otters frequent its waters.

Where navigable, the Bonnechere River, particularly in its northwest sections, offers lovely short excursions. Canoes can be put in the water at 1.2 km (0.7 mile) south of KM 30.6, at Little Norway Lake (KM 31.1), at KM 32.2, and at the point where the hydro line crosses the river (KM 34.3). It is also possible to launch a canoe outside the Park and paddle into it; one of the best locations for doing so is on Paugh Lake Road where it crosses the Bonnechere River 2 km (1.2 miles) past Turner's Camp. Another great location is Couchain Lake (KM 6.5).

Also, Basin and Foys lakes, the only sizeable bodies of water in this part of Algonquin, offer excellent half-day outings and wonderful Interior camping. Both have access roads that can be a bit rough to travel at times, so if you are in a car with low clearance you may wish to drive extra slowly. Foys Lake is the more remote of the two and has a beautiful campsite at the end of the road.

Although the Bonnechere is more a creek than a river in most of the Basin area, in the early years of the logging industry it was an important transportation route.

BRENT

Situated on beautiful Cedar Lake along the Petawawa River, Brent is the most developed access point in the northern part of Algonquin. It has an outfitting and supply store and a small drive-in campground with only basic facilities (i.e., no flush toilets or showers). The road into Brent, stretching 40 km (25 miles) from Deux-Rivieres on Highway 17, is unpaved but has been greatly improved in recent years. This is a good thing, because you drive more than 20 km (12.5 miles) before you even reach the Algonquin boundary.

Along the way there are several northern floating bogs that are just about as picture perfect as one can find anywhere. After these, there is a stretch of heavily logged forest (or forest remnants, to be more precise) on both sides of the road, a stark contrast to the scenic forest you drive through after you pass the Algonquin boundary.

Once in the Park you are soon immersed in a relatively young forest of yellow and white birches, balsam fir, red maple and trembling aspen. Watch for the "perched birches" – yellow birch growing as if on stilts (their elevated

The Brent Crater, just beyond the wall of trees, may be not seem impressive from this vantage point, but its story is a compelling one.

roots were exposed once the stump they were growing on decayed away). Near the Brent Crater Trail, the younger forest gives way to a tract of impressive hardwoods composed largely of sugar maples.

Currently, Brent is a mere shadow of its former existence. In earlier years, it was a thriving summer recreational and lumbering community. Long gone are the sawmill that was the heart of the lumbering industry here, the busy lodge and, in more recent years, the railway tracks themselves. There are two benefits to the disappearance of the rail line. No longer does the rumble of trains disrupt a camper's sleep in the nearby campground, and the abandoned rail line offers relatively easy and safe walking (no danger of being struck by a train).

The open nature of the Brent area provides ideal habitat for indigo buntings and mourning warblers, and its abundance of human structures so atypical of Algonquin is ideal for European starlings and chimney swifts. It is also a great spot for insect watching. Its large areas of orange and yellow hawkweeds, spreading dogbane and common milkweed are very popular with Canadian tiger swallowtails and other butterflies, and also attract day-flying hummingbird sphinx moths.

Apart from its access to Cedar Lake and the Petawawa River, the main highlight of this region is the Brent Crater Trail. This, the only interpretive trail in the northern part of the Park, is a unique one. It visits the crater formed when a meteorite crashed to Earth nearly 500 million years ago. The trail leads to the bottom of the crater, where evidence of the impact, such as shattered rocks, can be seen. The trail guide booklet discusses the clues that revealed the origin of the crater.

One interesting spin-off of the meteorite's impact is that limestone, a rare rock in Algonquin, is present here. Limestone contains calcium, which fuels the growth of calcareous plants otherwise rarely found in Algonquin. Some of these, such as bulblet fern, can be found right along the trail, especially at Post #3. A number of orchids, including northern green orchid and heart-leaved twayblade, grow in the low cedar woods that lie between the trail and Tecumseh Lake. This lake and Gilmour Lake both lie in the Crater and are unusual Park lakes because of their high bicarbonate content, which results from the geological history of the site. Be prepared for mosquitoes if you walk the trail in their season, for the low, damp ground is ideal habitat for these friendly creatures.

A lookout tower at the end of the trail where it meets the Brent Road affords a view of the opposite rim of the crater 4 km (2.5 miles) away. At time of writing, this tower was closed because of its aging timbers, but it is being rebuilt on the south side of the Brent Road.

The only place to see bulblet fern in Algonquin is on small exposures of lime-rich rock in the Brent Crater.

Also, many of the trees that grew alongside the trail were toppled in summer 2006 by a series of severe windstorms that were responsible for a massive blowdown that also affected a large section of forest on the south side of Gilmour Lake.

There is another site worth visiting. Along the lakeshore west of the Brent Store is a sizeable section of limestone escarpment, the only one in Algonquin. You can reach it either from the water (it is hidden behind shoreline cedars) or by walking a short trail that leads west from the boat launch west of the store, and then leaving the trail and heading toward the water.

The Brent Crater Trail alone makes this part of Algonquin worth a visit. If you plan to come specifically to visit the trail, I recommend you contact the Algonquin Park information office to enquire about the trail's condition.

Permits for day use and camping in Algonquin, as well as a few of the park publications, are sold at the Park office located on the Brent Road not far from Highway 17. Those who travelled to Brent in earlier days will recall that the office was formerly situated at the junction of the Brent and Wendigo Lake roads. The Brent Store offers a variety of food and camping supplies, as well as canoe rentals. At the time of writing, permits for renting a historic ranger cabin on the lake were also available at the store. The store is also a museum of sorts, with many historical artifacts and news clippings concerning the history of Brent on display.

Motorboats with a maximum 20 horsepower motor are allowed on Cedar Lake.

Hidden along the shore of Cedar Lake stands the only wall of sedimentary limestone in the Park.

All major access points, such as this one for Brent and Cedar lakes, have offices where permits are sold.

KIOSK

Kiosk is located on Kioshkokwi Lake, 48 km (30 miles) southwest of Mattawa on Highway 17. Highway 630, the 30.4 km (19-mile) access road from Highway 17, is paved.

At one time Kiosk was a busy town, with a sawmill, a school and numerous residents. The

sawmill, built in 1936, burnt down in 1973 and was rebuilt outside the Park. With the heart of this community gone, one after another, the families left. The once-thriving community of Kiosk is now a ghost town.

The office is at the lake, just past the railway tracks (this is the same inactive railway line that passes through Brent and Achray). Park permits are sold here, as well as a few publications. The small campground offers only basic facilities. Just west of the office stands a log building formerly a ranger cabin. This historic ranger cabin can be rented through Park Reservations (1-888-668-7275).

The Amable du Fond River flows out of Kiosk into the Ottawa. This is the only Algonquin river to flow northward, a reflection of the effect of the Algonquin dome.

Motorboats with motors up to 20 horsepower are allowed on Kioshkokwi Lake.

The Amable du Fond River flows north from Kiosk into the Ottawa River.

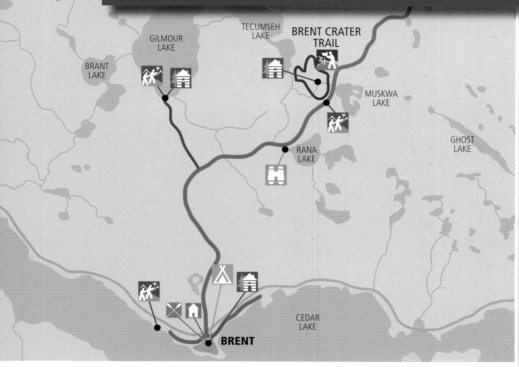

GILMOUR LAKE

TECUMSEH LAKE

BRENT CRATER TRAIL

BRANT LAKE

MUSKWA LAKE

GHOST LAKE

RANA LAKE

CEDAR LAKE

BRENT

 INTERPRETIVE TRAIL

 SCENIC VIEW

 HISTORIC SITE

 WILDLIFE VIEWING

 CAMPGROUND

 OUTFITTING STORE

 STORE RESTAURANT

 PHONE

 PERMITS/ INFORMATION

 LOGGING ROAD

 RAIL BED

 PARK BOUNDARY

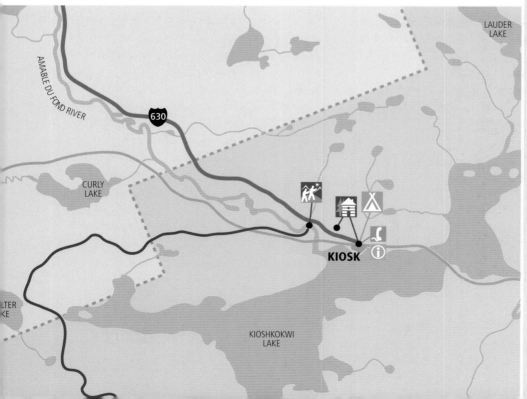

LAUDER LAKE

AMABLE DU FOND RIVER

630

CURLY LAKE

KIOSK

KIOSHKOKWI LAKE

...LTER ...KE

KINGSCOTE LAKE

The southern panhandle of Algonquin has until recently been one of the most under-utilized parts of the Park. Not that there was a lack of interesting natural features; the access road was in poor shape and there were few recreation options apart from canoeing or boating. However, this has changed. The road has been improved and several trails and a number of new campsites have been established. This southern region is well worth a visit (even a day excursion), as its hardwood forests harbour plants and animals that are rare in other parts of Algonquin, and there are some beautiful sites that can be accessed by foot, mountain bike or canoe, or on horseback.

There are two ways to enter this part of Algonquin. You can drive on an unpaved road to Kingscote Lake. This 7 km (4.4-mile) road leaves the Elephant Lake Road (County Road 10) 13 km (8 miles) north of Harcourt and 22 km (13.7 miles) west of Maynooth (where County Road 10 is called Peterson Road). You can also access the Park by foot, mountain bike or horse from the High Falls parking area, which lies along County Road 10, just 2 km (1.2 miles) east of the Kingscote Lake Road.

While Kingscote Lake may look like many other Algonquin lakes, it is different in terms of the plant and animal life found nearby. In early spring the hardwood forests surrounding the lake support a rich assortment of wildflowers that are either rare or not found farther north in the Park. From early spring, even before the wild leeks, blue cohosh and Canada violets have appeared, and right through to the end of summer, the piercing *keeee-yer, keeee-yer* calls of red-shouldered hawks can usually be heard from the lake. As many as three pairs of these snake-eating hawk, highly unusual anywhere else in Algonquin, nest near Kingscote Lake every summer.

The Kingscote Lake access point offers two types of campsites. On Kingscote and several neighbouring lakes, 23 Interior campsites are now accessible by canoe (motorboats with up to 20 horsepower motors are also allowed on Kingscote Lake). There are also six tenting campsites on the southwest corner of the lake, all situated within a short walking distance of a parking lot. These walk-in sites offer vault toilets, but no drinking water or shower facilities.

Terrific canoe day-trips can be initiated from Kingscote Lake. From the northeast corner of the lake you can portage into Upper and Lower Minnow lakes, or Big Rock Lake. If you are up to the 1300 m (1,420 yard) portage that takes you to Big Rock, you will be rewarded. The towering rock cliff for which this lake is named is spectacular. The map-brochure *Canoe Routes of Algonquin Provincial Park* is essential for any trip, as it details not only the portages but also the Interior campsites. Remember, a permit is required for camping, and sites must be reserved (1-888-668-7275).

Two hiking trails, accessible from Scorch Lake, usually require more than a day's paddle to reach. Leaving the southeast corner of the lake, the 1 km (0.6 mile) Scorch Lake Lookout Trail offers a great view of the lake. Branching off from this trail is the Bruton Farm Hiking Trail (2.5 km/1.5 miles). This trail brings you to the site of the Bruton Depot Farm, which was established in 1875. A 37 metre (120-foot) steel fire tower, built in the mid-1930s, stood here as well.

MAP 18
OTHER ACCESS POINTS

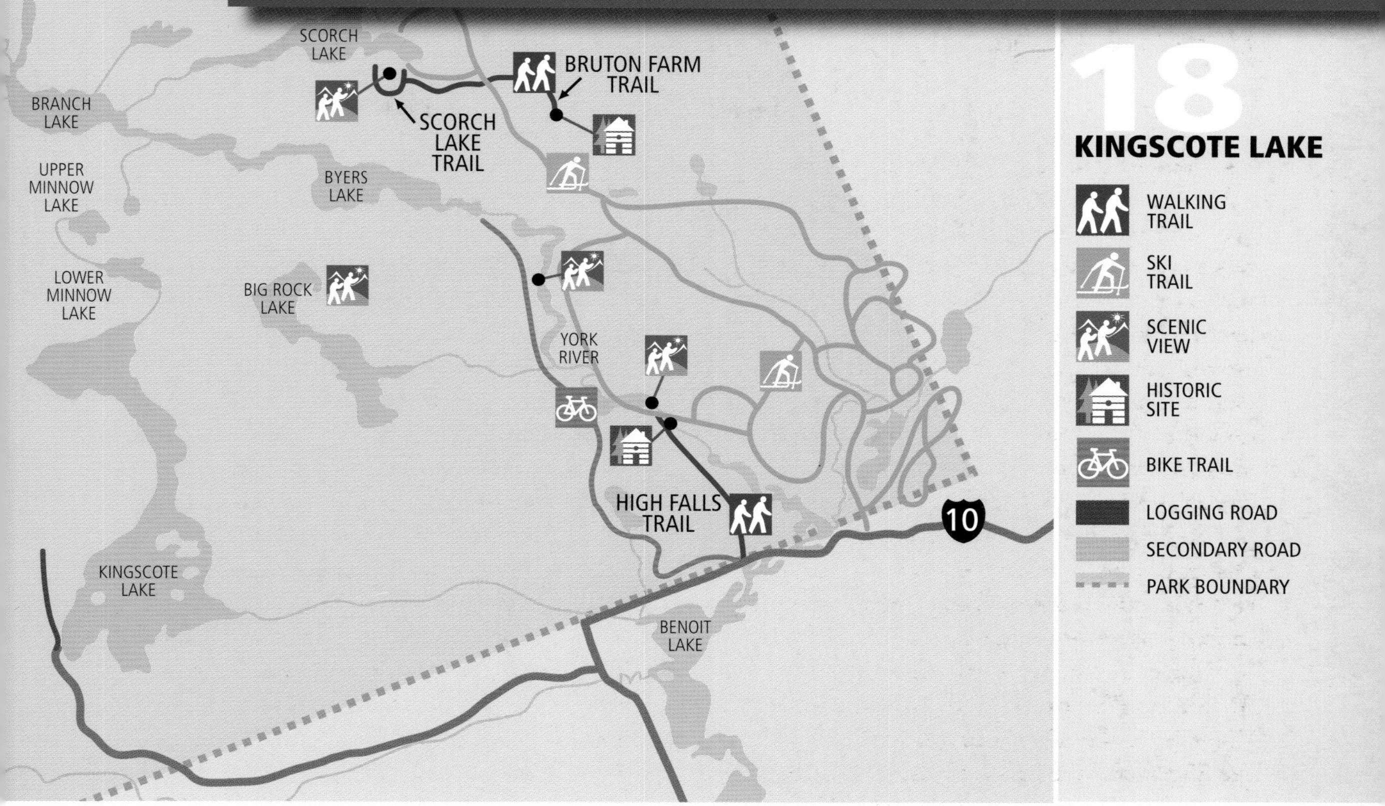

SCORCH
LAKE

BRANCH
LAKE

UPPER
MINNOW
LAKE

BYERS
LAKE

LOWER
MINNOW
LAKE

BIG ROCK
LAKE

BRUTON FARM
TRAIL

SCORCH
LAKE
TRAIL

YORK
RIVER

HIGH FALLS
TRAIL

KINGSCOTE
LAKE

BENOIT
LAKE

18

KINGSCOTE LAKE

WALKING
TRAIL

SKI
TRAIL

SCENIC
VIEW

HISTORIC
SITE

BIKE TRAIL

LOGGING ROAD

SECONDARY ROAD

PARK BOUNDARY

A horseback-riding trail leads past the Bruton Farm to Lostwater Lake. This trail originates opposite the High Falls parking lot, from which two other trails also start. For more information on horseback riding, call South Algonquin Trails at 1-800-758-4801.

The High Falls Hiking Trail is a very easy trail that covers less than 2 km (1.2 miles) round trip. The first section of the trail is quite level and follows an old road through a pine plantation. The next section is a footpath leading to the York River. The long rock piles at the base of the rapids are historic glance piers that prevented logs from going ashore during spring log drives. Farther upstream is the magnificent High Falls, at its best in spring but still worth a visit at any time of year.

The Byers Lake Mountain Bike Trail, a round-trip trail (13 km/8 miles), is not particularly difficult since it follows an old logging road. Approximately two-thirds of the way to Byers Lake, the Gut Rapids Spur Hiking Trail leads east to the York River. Bikes are prohibited on this short, looped trail. At Gut Rapids the river flows through a steep, narrow canyon, a must-see for anyone using the bike trail.

Day-use and camping permits, as well the Algonquin South brochure (with maps for all the trails), the *Canoe Routes of Algonquin Provincial Park* map-brochure and other publications, are available at Pine Grove Point (705-448-2387), located a short distance east of the junction of the Kingscote Lake access point road and County Road 10 (well marked with signs).

OTHER ACCESS POINTS

In addition to the main access areas profiled above, Algonquin Park can also be entered via a number of other entrance points. Most of these are used primarily for canoe access to the vast Interior and offer few services apart from a permit office and a parking area. Details about the remaining access points can be found in *Canoe Routes of Algonquin Provincial Park*, a map-brochure available at all retail outlets in the Park, or by mail from the Friends of Algonquin (see page 215 for address).

The majority of the access points serve as starting points for longer canoe trips into the Park Interior. With more than 1800 km (1,100 miles) of possible routes, the Park Interior boasts a vast number of points of interest, both historical and natural. The discussion of all of the known sites would require a massive book (or books) and is beyond the scope and intent of this guide. A brief listing of a few of the Interior highlights follows the description of four popular access points.

Historic ranger cabins, such as this one at Kitty Lake, can be rented for overnight or longer stays.

RAIN LAKE

Rain Lake access point is located 35 km (22 miles) east of Highway 11. The access road is unpaved, and the small campground has only basic facilities. The access point office sells permits and a few publications.

This access point offers a rentable historic ranger cabin. Bookings must be made through Ontario Park Reservations (1-888-668-7275).

Rain Lake provides access not only to canoe routes but also to the Western Uplands Backpacking Trail. Motorboats with motors to a maximum of 10 horsepower are allowed on this lake.

SHALL LAKE

Shall Lake lies 24 km (15 miles) north of Madawaska on Highway 60. The access road is for the most part unpaved. There are no drive-in campgrounds or other facilities here, except for the office that sells permits and a few publications.

The highlights here, though, are the easy canoe routes that can be accessed from Shall Lake. Some very scenic lakes, such as Shirley and Booth, can be reached with only minimal portaging. Many historic sites, including a ranger cabin on Kitty Lake, are within easy access. A total of 10 "paddle-in" campsites (campsites located a short distance from a drive-in location) are situated on Crotch Lake, only minutes of paddling time from the canoe launch.

Motorboats are not allowed on these waters.

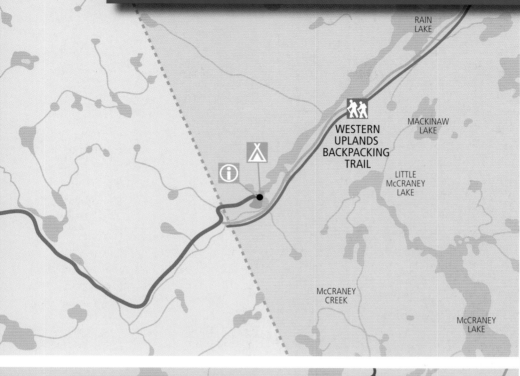

RAIN LAKE

MACKINAW LAKE

WESTERN UPLANDS BACKPACKING TRAIL

LITTLE McCRANEY LAKE

McCRANEY CREEK

McCRANEY LAKE

19
RAIN LAKE

 CANOE OUTING

 HIKING TRAIL

 CAMPGROUND

 PERMITS/ INFORMATION

 LOGGING ROAD

 OLD RAILWAY LINE

 HYDRO LINE

PARK BOUNDARY

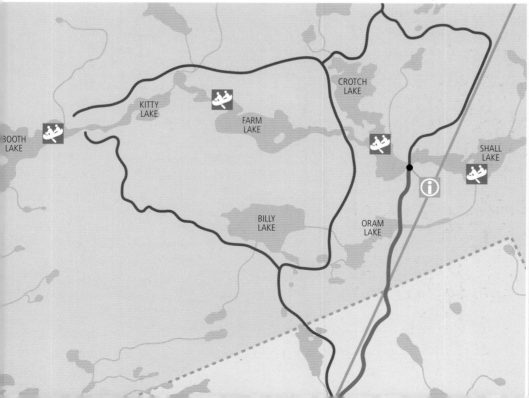

KITTY LAKE

CROTCH LAKE

FARM LAKE

BOOTH LAKE

SHALL LAKE

BILLY LAKE

ORAM LAKE

20
SHALL LAKE

THE PARK INTERIOR

A canoe trip lasting several days or longer gives one the opportunity to really experience Algonquin. Awakening in a dew-covered tent to the sleepy whistles of a white-throated sparrow allows you to savour the new day as thousands of earlier explorers have done. To watch a setting sun set the waters ablaze while the rising wails of loons echo off distant hills is to discover the essence of the Park. Camping in the Park Interior bonds you with the wild in an intimate and unequalled way.

You need be neither an expert canoeist nor an experienced camper to explore the Park Interior. Common sense and preparation are the only requirements. Outfitters are usually willing to advise not only on what equipment will best suit your needs but also on which routes might be within your time budget. Park Interpretive staff members are also generally well versed in Interior travel and are worth consulting for advice. *The Canoeist's Manual*, produced by the Friends of Algonquin Park, is an excellent practical aid for learning the basics of canoeing.

Designated campsites are situated along most waterways throughout the Interior. Each has a fire pit as well as a privy of some sort. A maximum of nine people are permitted to camp at a single site. As all access points have a limit to the number of parties permitted entry each day, it is recommended to reserve well in advance. The number is provided in the "Useful Services" (page 211). The permit offices for each access point are listed in the map-brochure *Canoe Routes of Algonquin Provincial Park*. Remember that in the Interior, cans and bottles are banned.

A different way to experience the Park Interior is by dog sled in winter. The Sunday Lake Dog Sled Trail starts at the Big Pines Trail on Highway 60. Outward Bound Canda offers dog sledding expeditions on this trail. Algonquin-way Tours offer trips that vary from 10 to 66 km (6–40 miles) in length. Chocpaw Expeditions offers longer outings ranging in length from 45 to 65 km (27–40 miles) on the North Algonquin Dog Sled Trail, which starts near South River. Trail maps are available at both East and West gates, and by contacting the Park Information office.

"Tips for the Explorer" (page 203) offers a few basic camping guidelines. *Canoe Routes of Algonquin Provincial Park* is certainly a must for both navigating and camping through the Interior. Beyond this, it is also an important tool for enhancing a canoe trip, as it identifies areas of natural history and historical interest. Another useful park publication concerning Interior use is the free tabloid *Algonquin Information Guide*. Two helpful and enjoyable books foranyone interested in canoe-tripping in Algonquin are Don Lloyd's *Canoeing Algonquin Park* and Kevin Callan's *A Paddler's Guide to Algonquin Park*.

A trip into the Park Interior brings you close to the heart of the wilderness.

WILDLIFE-VIEWING AREAS

 Wildlife can certainly be encountered on any Interior trip but some areas are better for certain species in particular. The following is a brief summary of good locations for seeing animals.

- ## Hailstorm Creek

  This extensive boggy creek lies at the northwest corner of Opeongo Lake. It can be a bit of a challenge to get there, for Opeongo is the largest lake in Algonquin and can be exceedingly windy and rough at times. The Opeongo Store offers guided excursions to see wildlife here. You are taken by water taxi to the north end of the lake where the creek can be accessed – a safe and efficient way of getting there. You then enter the shallow creek, a favoured moose-feeding area, by canoe (motors are not allowed in the creek). I have seen as many as 24 moose at one time feeding here. Early summer is certainly the best time to see these giants. Hailstorm Creek is also an excellent place to view river otters.

  Another feature of this and the following large bog has been the presence of nesting bobolinks and savannah sparrows, birds typically found in farmland outside the Park. In recent years these have been harder to find, while another species has become more regular. Sandhill cranes, huge birds with a loud bugling call, are now being seen here and likely nest. Reports of sandhill cranes and any other unusual birds should be sent to the Park Naturalist at the Visitor Centre.

- ## Grassy Bay

  This boggy creek extending west from the south end of Trout Lake is similar to Hailstorm Creek in habitat, but is less productive for moose.

- ## Tim River

  This meandering river on the west side of the Park is excellent for moose in early summer. It also harbours river otters as well as many species of northern birds.

- ## Nipissing River

  Like the Tim River, this winding waterway is excellent for moose and river otters. The stretch between Cedar and Nadine lakes is particularly good.

- ## Catfish Lake

  This lake is an important one for moose-calving in spring (mid-May) and is also important as a feeding area in early summer. The large boggy marsh between Catfish and Sunfish lakes is excellent in summer.

- ## McCarthy Creek

  This creek lies at the southwest corner of Booth Lake. Virtually every species of aquatic plant known in Algonquin is present here. This rich array attracts moose in early summer.

- ## Hogan Lake

  The huge boggy marsh at the southwest end is an excellent summer feeding site for moose.

OTHER AREAS OF NATURAL SIGNIFICANCE

Here is a short list of some of the more outstanding areas of natural significance.

- ## Crow River White Pines

  This is one of only two areas that still have virgin white pines standing. These magnificent 35 metre (115-foot) trees tower above the nearby hardwoods. The pine stand is located approximately 2 km (1.5 miles) south of the Crow River just east of Crow Lake.

- ### Dividing Lake White Pines
  This is the other area where virgin white pines still grow. Dividing Lake is situated on the southwest border of Algonquin, south of Smoke and Ragged lakes.

- ### Dickson Lake Red Pines
  While not as tall as the virgin white pines at Crow and Dividing lakes, the red pines growing on the east side of Dickson Lake are the oldest trees in Algonquin. They are presently more than 340 years old.

POINTS OF HISTORICAL INTEREST

There is such a vast number of logging camp ruins and other relics from the early days in the Park that an entire volume would be needed to cover all of the points of historical interest. Many of these have either become next to impossible to find or can be reached only with extreme effort. Ranger cabins were used in the early 1900s as stopovers for Park rangers during their patrols for poachers and fires. Many were intentionally destroyed in earlier years but some of the few remaining, such as those on Kitty and McKaskill lakes, have been repaired and can now be rented by the night or by the week. This can be done only by reservation (Ontario Park Reservations) from the last weekend in April to noon on Friday of the Thanksgiving weekend. For more information, call the Park information services.

The following is simply a listing of a few of the more obvious structures that one can find relatively easily during Interior trips:

Burntroot Lake Alligator
The remains of one of these amphibious logging vessels rest on the southwest shore of Burntroot Lake. The remnants of the Barnet Depot Farm, first inhabited in 1892, are also situated here.

Catfish Lake Alligator
Parts of an alligator are visible on the island in the northeast corner of Catfish Lake.

Dennison Farm (East Arm of Opeongo Lake)
Captain John Dennison cleared this farm in the 1870s. He was killed in 1881 by a black bear caught in a trap, and was buried at the farm. The Dennison family moved out of the Park in 1882. The Fraser Lumber Company took over the farm and ran it far a number of years as a depot farm.

Dufond Farm (Manitou Lake)
Ignace and Francis Dufond cleared this site in 1888 and sold produce to logging operations. This farm, the last one in the Park to have been privately owned, was abandoned in 1916.

Barnet Depot (Burntroot Lake)
Depots were the administrative and supply headquarters for logging companies. Farms were frequently established at these sites to grow potatoes for the men, and oats and hay for the horses.

This depot was built in 1890 by the Barnet Lumber Company and was used until at least 1912. A root cellar and the remains of an alligator can still be easily located.

McLachlin Depot (Trout Lake)
At the northeast corner of Trout Lake lie the remains of this depot, built around 1900 by the McLachlin Lumber Company.

GENERAL CAMPING

This section may be useful in providing a few basic tips for this popular Algonquin activity. Please refer to "Relevant Publication" (page 215) for specialized books dealing with camping in more detail.

Campsites such as this one on Fork Lake offer a peaceful refuge from today's fast-paced life.

General Camping Etiquette

Algonquin is becoming an increasingly popular place for visitors to explore. Unfortunately, there are always a few truly inconsiderate campers who leave campsites, portages and trails in unsightly messes. This kind of user is virtually impossible to educate. However, unthinking acts are sometimes performed simply out of ignorance. It is these unconscious acts that might be reduced with a little bit of knowledge about camping etiquette. Here are some general rules to follow:

Beauty pervades every inch of Algonquin, whether it be a lakeside campsite or the banks of a meandering stream.

- Never cut live trees down for firewood. Sufficient wood can always be gathered from fallen branches or dead trees. In the public campgrounds wood can be purchased. You can also bring your own supply to the drive-in campsites.

- Use the facilities provided at campgrounds or campsites for your "washroom deposits." If you are in dire straits (for example, the "mood" strikes while you're on a trail or portage), then make sure you go off the trail and scrape a shallow depression in the ground. When you have finished, cover up all evidence with soil and leaves.

- Never leave garbage at a site, thinking that someone else will pack it out for you. Pack out all non-burnable items. And remember, cans and bottles are prohibited in the Park Interior.

- Use biodegradable soaps and shampoos on camping trips.

- Never wash your dishes in lakes or rivers. Do this away from the water's edge.

- Since sound travels so well at night, think of other campers when you feel moved to strike up a loud conversation or play that musical instrument.

- If possible, if you do encounter someone else's trash and you have room in your pack for it, consider carrying it out as well.

- Never start a fire outside of a designated fire pit and never leave a fire burning unattended.

Choosing a Site

Although camping in Algonquin can be broken down into two basic types – drive-in and Interior – site choices are available for each. Along Highway 60, the campgrounds vary tremendously in the facilities they offer as well as in their general environment. Too often a person grabs the first available campsite, only to find out that another choice may have been preferable.

Never set up a tent in a depression in the ground. It can – and certainly does – rain in Algonquin, and low sites (as are frequently found in Lake of Two Rivers Campground) may fill up with water after a period of heavy rain. When choosing a site for a tent, try to choose a slightly elevated, level area to pitch it on. If rain is anticipated, a heel-dug trench around the tent may help direct surface water away.

On Interior trips, island campsites generally are preferable for a couple of reasons. As a rule, they tend to experience more wind and therefore have fewer problems with biting insects. Bears are usually absent. Also, islands frequently offer enhanced aesthetics in terms of sunrise and sunset viewing.

Remember, Interior camping may only take place on designated sites.

Equipment

Since an excellent treatment of camping equipment is covered in specific books, such as Kevin Callan's *The Happy Camper*, I offer only a few tips here.

A portable camp stove is a must for any camping trip. For drive-in camping, larger multi-burner stoves with large fuel tanks are commonly used. For Interior trips, smaller single-burner backpacking stoves are preferred. The Coleman Peak series, MSR Whisperlite and Optimus stoves are good examples. A camp stove is essential for any backpacking or canoeing trip not only because of the chances of bad weather but also because of the possibility of a fire ban in the drier summer season.

Also very useful is a water filter pump. In days gone by, chemical treatment or boiling were the only ways to guarantee safe drinking water. Today there are a number of extremely lightweight water filter pumps that screw onto a Nalgene bottle, another very useful item to bring along.

To boil water, I now use a Kelly Kettle. This is a remarkable lightweight kettle apparently invented by Irish fishermen who could find scant fuel on the islands they stopped at. The kettle is a cone with a hollow wall that holds the water. A small fire in the base sends the heat up through the inner part of the cone, heating the walls and the water in the process. All you do is drop a few twigs down the open centre as the fuel burns up. A handful of twigs (with a few scraps of birch bark as starter) are all that is needed to get a cup or two of water boiling in mere minutes. As far as I am aware, Lee Valley Tools was the first to sell this ingenious kettle.

For Interior camping, no trip is complete without a good length of rope, toilet paper, flashlight with new batteries, first aid kit, waterproof matches and either a *Canoe Routes of Algonquin Provincial Park* or a *Backpacking Trails of Algonquin Provincial Park* map-brochure.

Zip-lock bags seem to have been invented for Interior tripping, for they can be used to keep maps, toilet paper and food dry. Although waterproof matches can be purchased, I still take the precaution of putting them (along with their striking pad) and regular strike-anywhere matches in airtight containers. Today, all sorts and sizes of lightweight and airtight plastic food containers are available to carry anything you wish to bring.

Although a light camping axe can be a useful piece of equipment, I frequently go on shorter trips without one. A folding camp saw is lighter to pack and occupies less space than an axe – and really is more practical. Since the bulk of firewood used is usually branch-sized, a saw is all that is needed to cut up the wood. For more extended trips I pack both a saw and an axe. After a day or two of hard rain, much of the smaller wood gets soaked. I use my saw to cut up small blocks of wood from larger fallen trunks, then use my axe to split these to access the drier wood inside.

When on an Interior trip, one very important rule is not only to keep the matches dry but also to keep your sleeping bag free of moisture. While many stuff bags are reasonably waterproof, I still package my sleeping bag inside a double garbage bag to help ensure its dryness.

The One-match Fire

Whether you are camping in a drive-in public campground or on an Interior campsite on a remote island, the mechanics of successfully starting a campfire are the same. All too often, an eager camper attempts to ignite chunks of wood the size of a tree trunk. The best strategy is to start small and only add larger pieces of wood after the fire is established. Most cooking fires actually require wood no thicker than a pencil!

Open fires are allowed unless a fire ban has been declared because of an excessively hot, dry period. As a precaution, make sure you bring a camping stove with you, particularly if you are heading for the Park Interior. Fires must be set only inside the fire pit located at every designated camping spot. If the pit is full of loose ash from previous fires, clean it out before you prepare your fuel.

Before building the fire, make sure you have collected adequate fuel. (If you are in a public campground, wood is sold at designated places and times.) Never cut living trees for wood. Even the most heavily used Interior sites will have sufficient starting fuel in the vicinity of the fire pit. And I often find enough small material to get a good fire going.

Start off with a base of loose, easily ignited material. If you have waste paper with you, this will suffice. I find that small strips of white birch bark (which can usually be found lying on the ground or can be taken from logs or dead trees – never from living trees!) work extremely well. If neither is available, dry pine needles and/or knife shavings from a dry stick will do. On top of this, add fine twigs. The best to use are the very fine dead twigs found on the bottom branches of coniferous trees such as spruce and balsam fir. These also can usually be found on the ground. If you are in a campground, use an axe to split off thin slivers of wood (alias "kindling"). A couple of handfuls are usually enough. On top of this, add larger twigs and small branches (or larger pieces of split wood) to form a rough pyramid. Now strike your match and light the base. Unless you are making an evening's-end fire, the largest size of wood pieces required should be the same size as the last ones you added to this fuel pile.

If a strong wind is blowing, build a windbreak out of stones. A strategically placed pack will also

The Algonquin Visitor Centre offers one of the finest panoramas in the Park year round.

help reduce the effect of the breeze. Never build a large fire under very windy conditions. It is best to use your camp stove when such conditions arise.

When it comes time to call it a day, be sure to put out your fire. While it may be calm when you retire to the tent, a wind could easily spring up overnight. Never leave a site while a fire is still burning or coals are still glowing. Thoroughly dowse the pit with water to ensure that no accidents happen.

Wood can be purchased at drive-in campgrounds, but there is nothing wrong with bringing your own supply.

Food

Perhaps the most important rule is never to have a messy campsite. Food scraps, dirty dishes, exposed food – and even coolers left lying around – serve to attract a variety of animals, including black bears. If you are staying in a drive-in campground, place all waste material in the provided bear-proof garbage structures. Never bring food into your tent, for the odours will linger, possibly attracting a hungry scavenger. Make sure food is not left on the tables and that coolers are stored in your vehicle trunk (with lid closed!) overnight or when you are away from the site. If you are staying at an Interior site, burn all burnable leftovers and place non-burnables with your food in a pack hung well off the ground. (Remember, cans and bottles are prohibited in the Park Interior.)

Anyone staying at a site without a vehicle should have the food hung out of reach of animals. I usually bring at least one 10 metre (30-foot) rope on all Interior trips. Pines with a stout lower limb projecting out from the trunk at least 4 metres (13 feet) above the ground are ideal for hanging packs. If you have difficulty throwing the rope over a branch, try weighting it with a piece

of wood or a stone.

Sometimes, if a suitable tree can't be found, two ropes are necessary. One length can be suspended between two adjacent trees and the other piece hung over it. However, single trees are far simpler for hanging packs and a bit of searching near the site will usually turn one up.

The pack should be hung at least 3 metres (10 feet) off the ground and at least 1 metre (3 feet) from the trunk. Never leave your food in a pack on the ground, in the canoe or in the tent overnight – or when you are away from the campsite.

The type of food you bring to the Park depends primarily on the type of camping you choose. Drive-in campgrounds allow virtually any type of food. Canoeists and backpackers must pack lighter and less easily spoiled foods. As well, Interior users are not permitted to pack cans or bottles. Excellent suggestions for types of foods to bring can be found on the back of the *Canoe Routes of Algonquin Provincial Park* map-brochure (the essential publication for any Park canoe trip) and in Kevin Callan's *The Happy Camper*. My list of essentials for camping trips includes instant oatmeal, powdered skim milk, multigrain bagels, peanut butter, honey, tea bags and dry pasta.

When walking a trail that exceeds 2 km (1.5 miles) in length, it is wise to bring a bit of food and water to get you through the trip.

Water

Drive-in campgrounds have treated water available. For Interior trips, water from untreated sources must be used. Many campers, including myself, take water from larger lakes and use it untreated. This is generally a safe practice if you take water from a distance away from the shore and down as far as the hand can reach. However, there is always a remote chance of contacting giardia or "beaver fever" by drinking untreated water. Thus, many campers use filtration systems or purification tablets, which are available at any camping or outfitting store. Today there are fantastic water filtration systems that use ceramic filters. They are compact, lightweight, and attach to a Nalgene bottle for easy use.

Boiling water will also make it safe to drink, but you must wait for quite a while if you want a cool drink. Backpackers should carry water with them, replenishing reserves if necessary when they come to lakes. Regardless of where you are in the Park, never drink untreated water from beaver ponds or peatlands.

Clothing

Because of Algonquin's elevations, the nights can be surprisingly cool, even cold, in late spring and even mid-summer. If you are camping in drive-in locations, the best strategy is to bring a heavy sweater or jacket, and perhaps even a light parka, especially in August. If you are camping in the Interior, then several layers of clothes might be preferable to a heavy parka. Layers of loose clothes tend to be warmer (each layer traps air) than one heavier garment. A T-shirt, a heavier long-sleeved cotton shirt, a light sweater and an outer windbreaker should suffice quite nicely. The beauty of layering is that you can mix and match to suit the temperatures.

Be sure to bring rainwear no matter where you camp – otherwise you may have to wear wet clothes or stay inside the tent until the rain ends (which could be several days!). One important consideration is colour. During fly season (see "Biting Insects," page 82) light colours such as tan or pale yellow are much better than dark colours, especially blue or black.

Footwear should consist of shoes with good treads for walking trails or portages. Although hiking boots may seem to be the ideal wear for Algonquin, as far as most people are concerned, including myself, they are not necessary. Comfortable hiking shoes or sturdy running shoes normally suffice. The important thing is to bring a spare pair to wear in case one pair gets wet. If you have weak ankles and are concerned about sprained ankles, then hiking boots might offer better support. However, travelling an Algonquin trail is not like climbing the Rocky Mountains (although users of the Centennial Ridges Trail might care to differ!).

Currently, rubber shoes called "Crocs" are becoming very popular with canoeists for they are lightweight and dry quickly when wet. However, when I canoe or if I go into wet terrain such as bogs, I like to wear old runners with neoprene socks and cotton liners on my feet. I have seen cases where Crocs pull off in muddy bottoms or plant material gets stuck between the foot and the shoe, causing some discomfort.

Cell Phones

In recent years the use of cell phones has become chronic in our society. Not having one myself, I can only report what others have told me about their use in Algonquin. A few rather unsightly towers erected along Highway 60 permit the use of these phones in close proximity to that highway only, with a few areas remaining "dead zones." On the East Side, a transmission tower erected beside the Sand Lake gate allows use of phones within close proximity to it.

Because of the rocky nature of the Park, however, cell phones do not work in the Park Interior. This to me is a very good thing, for I cannot imagine having my enjoyment of the calls of a loon interrupted by the ring of a phone! If one feels the need to keep in touch with the outside world during a canoe trip into the Interior, at the time of writing a satellite phone is necessary.

OUTFITTING SERVICES

For outfitters inside the Park, the lake on which they are situated is given in brackets. For those outside the Park, the general area of Algonquin nearest to the outfitters is given in bracket. Where available, contact information, including website, is listed. If one is not provided for a facility that interests you, a web search will likely result in more information.

Outfitters Located Inside Algonquin

Algonquin Outfitters (Cedar Lake)
R.R. #1, Highway 60
Dwight, ON P0A 1H0
705-635-2243 or 1-800-469-4948
www.algonquinoutfitters.com

Opeongo Store/Algonquin Outfitters (Opeongo Lake)
R.R. #1, Highway 60
Dwight, ON P0A 1H0
613-637-2075 or 1-888-280-8886
www.algonquinoutfitters.com

The Portage Store (Canoe Lake)
c/o Huntsville P.O.
Huntsville, ON P0A 1K0
705-633-5662
www.portagestore.com
info@portagestore.com

Outfitters Outside Algonquin

Algonquin Bound (Highway 60, Basin Depot)
613-637-5508 or 1-800-704-4537
www.algonquinbound.com
info@algonquinbound.com

Algonquin North (Kiosk)
Highway 17 and Highway 630
1-877-544-3544
canoe@algonquinnorth.com
www.algonquinnorth.com

Algonquin Outfitters (Highway 60)
R.R. #1, Highway 60
Dwight, ON P0A 1H0
705-635-2243 or 1-800-469-4948
www.algonquinoutfitters.com

Algonquin Portage Limited (East Side, Brent)
1352 Barron Canyon Road
Pembroke, ON K8A 6W7
613-735-1795
www.algonquinportage.com
portage@nrtco.net

Canoe Algonquin (western Algonquin)
P.O. Box 224
Kearney, ON P0A 1H0
705-636-5956 or 1-800-818-1210
www.canoealgonquin.com

Northern Wilderness Outfitters (northwestern Algonquin)
P.O. Box 89
South River, ON P0A 1X0
705-386-0466
www.northernwilderness.com
info@northernwilderness.com

Opeongo Outfitters (Highway 60)
P.O. Box 123
Whitney, ON K0J 2M0
613-637-5470 or 1-800-790-1864
ww.opeongooutfitters.com

Algonquin in the autumn is a lively mosaic of blazing hardwoods and cool, dark conifers.

Outfitters Outside Algonquin (continued)

Valley Ventures Canoe Outfitting (Brent, East Side)
P.O. Box 1115
33861 Highway 17
Deep River, ON K0J 1P0
613-584-9016
www.valleyvent.ca
vent@magma.ca

Voyageur Outfitting (western Algonquin)
P.O. Box 69
South River, ON P0A 1X0
1-877-837-8889
dmacvoy@primus.ca
www.voyageuroutfitting.com

ACCOMMODATION

Only lodges and motels found either inside Algonquin Park or within 20 km (12 miles) of the Park are listed here. Of course, many places beyond this arbitrary distance also offer accommodation. Nearby cities within an hour's drive to Algonquin Park include Huntsville to the west of the Park, North Bay and Deep River to the north, Petawawa and Pembroke to the northeast, Barry's Bay, Wilno and Killaloe to the east, and Bancroft to the south. Each city has its website that will link you to local accommodations. Additionally, the Algonquin Park website link, www.algonquinpark.on.ca/service, will offer alternatives to the services listed below, as will the website www.cottage-resort.com/ontario-algonquin.htm. The Ontario Ministry of Tourism website, www.tourism.gov.on.ca, is also worth a visit when planning a trip to Algonquin.

Accommodation Inside Algonquin Park

Arowhon Pines Lodge
P.O. Box 10001
Huntsville, ON P1H 2G5
705-633-5661 or 1-866-633-5661
www.arowhonpines.ca
resort@arowhonpines.ca

Bartlett Lodge
P.O. Box 10004
Huntsville, ON P1H 2G8
705-633-5543 or 1-866-614-5355
www.bartlettlodge.com
bartlett@globalserve.net

Killarney Lodge
P.O. Box 10005
Algonquin Park, ON P1H 2G9
705-633-5551 or 1-866-473-5551
www.killarneylodge.com
info@killarneylodge.com

Accommodation Outside Algonquin Park
West of Algonquin

Algonquin Lakeside Inn
R.R. #1, Dwight, ON P0A 1H0
705-635-2434 or 1-800-387-2244
www.algonquininn.com
stay@algonquininn.com

Blue Spruce Resort
R.R. #1, Dwight, ON P0A 1H0
705-635-2330
www.bluespruce.ca
info@bluespruce.ca

Clover Leaf Cottages
Oxtongue Lake Road
Dwight, ON P0A 1H0
705-635-2049

Dwight Village Motel
2801 Highway 60
Dwight, ON P0A 1H0
705-635-2400
www.dwightvillagemotel.com
info@dwightvillagemotel.com

Lakewoods Cottage Resort
R.R. #1, Oxtongue Lake, ON P0A 1H0
705-635-2087
www.lakewoods-resort.net
vacation@lakewoods-resort.net

Logging Chain Lodge
2840 Highway 69
P.O. Box 170
Dwight, ON P0A 1H0
705-635-2575 or 1-877-635-2575
www.loggingchainlodge.on.ca
info@loggingchainlodge.on.ca

Nor'Loch Lodge Resort
P.O. Box 40
Dwight, ON P0A 1H0
705-635-2231 or 1-800-565-2231
www.norloch.com

Oxtongue Lake Cottages
R.R. #1, Dwight, ON P0A 1H0
705-635-2951
brian@muskoka.com

Parkway Cottage Resort
4412 Highway 60
Dwight, ON P0A 1H0
705-635-2763
www.parkwayresort.ca
parkway_resort@yahoo.ca

Riverside Motel/Restaurant
P.O. Box 94
Dwight, ON P0A 1H0
705-635-1677
www.riverside-motel.ca

Spring Lake Resort
R.R. #1, Dwight, ON P0A 1H0
705-635-1562 or 1-800-461-1997
www.springlakeresort.on.ca
springlk@sympatico.ca

White Birches Cottage Resort
R.R. #1, Dwight, ON P0A 1H0
705-635-2322 or 1-800-263-4794
www.whitebirches-algonquin.com
whitebirches@accglobal.net

Wolf Den Bunkhouse
4568 Highway 60
Oxtongue Lake, ON P0A 1H0
705-635-9336 or 1-866-271-9336
www.wolfdenbunkhouse.com
wden@wolfdenbunkhouse.com

East of Algonquin Park

Algonquin Area Bed and Breakfast
Whitney, ON K0J 2M0
613-637-5387

Algonquin East Gate Motel
P.O. Box 193
Whitney, ON K0J 2M0
613-637-2652
www.algonquineastgatemotel.com
eastgatemotel@nexicom.net

Algonquin Parkway Inn
P.O. Box 237
Whitney, ON K0J 2M0
613-637-2760

Algonquin Portage Limited
1352 Barron Canyon Road
Pembroke, ON K8A 6W7
613-735-1795
www.algonquinportage.com
portage@nrtco.net

All Star Resort
Madawaska, ON K0J 2C0
613-637-5592
www.allstarresort.com
info@allstarresort.com

Bear Trail Adventure Lodge
P.O. Box 310
Whitney, ON K0J 2M0
613-637-5507
www.adventurelodge.com
info@adventurelodge.com

The Couples Resort
P.O. Box 310
Galeairy Lake Road
Whitney, ON K0J 2M0
613-637-2662
www.couplesresort.ca

Hay Lake Lodge
P.O. Box 189
Whitney, ON K0J 2M0
613-637-2675
www.haylakecanada.com

East of Algonquin Park (continued)

The Mad Musher Restaurant and Lodge
P.O. Box 89
Whitney, ON K0J 2M0
613-637-2820 or 1-866-551-5534
www.madmusher.com
info@madmusher.com

Pine Grove Point
P.O. Box 121
Harcourt, ON K0L 1X0
705-448-2387
www.pinegrovepoint.com
pinegrovepoint@sympatico.ca

Riverland Lodge
P.O. Box 98
Madawaska, ON K0J 2C0
613-637-5338 or 1-800-701-8055
www.riverlandlodge.com
info@riverlandlodge.com

Riverview Cottages
P.O. Box 29
Galeairy Lake Road
Whitney, ON K0J 2M0
613-637-2690 or 1-88-387-9440
www.riverviewcottages.com

Whitney Cabins
P.O. Box 15
Whitney, ON K0J 2M0
613-637-1103

USEFUL ADDRESSES AND PHONE NUMBERS

Algonquin Visitor Centre
(613) 637-2828
www.algonquinpark.on.ca

Algonquin Provincial Park
Park Superintendent
Algonquin Provincial Park
Ministry of Natural Resources
P.O. Box 219
Whitney, ON K0J 2M0
(613) 637-2780
www.algonquinpark.on.ca

Camping Reservations
1-888-668-7275
outside Canada and USA: (519) 826-5290
www.OntarioParks.com

The Friends of Algonquin Park
P.O. Box 248
Whitney, ON K0J 2M0
(613) 637-2828
www.algonquinpark.on.ca

Park Information
(705) 633-5572
www.algonquinpark.on.ca

EMERGENCY TELEPHONE NUMBERS

Ontario Provincial Police
1-888-310-1122

Ambulance
Huntsville: 705-789-9694
Barry's Bay: 613-756-3090

Hospital
Barry's Bay Hospital: 613-756-3044
Huntsville Hospital: 705-789-2311

Ontario Poison Control
1-800-267-1373

Forest Fire
Pembroke: 1-800-853-4937
Haliburton: 1-888-239-4565

Towing / Auto Repair Services

Mochulla Auto Service (CAA)
Whitney, ON
613-637-2752 or 1-800-829-0906

Pretty's Towing
Herman's Road, Dwight, ON
705-635-2173 or 1-800-410-7114

APPENDIX 2 –
RELEVANT PUBLICATIONS

The following is a list of publications that deal with Algonquin Park. Many other excellent publications are now out of print; only those currently available are listed. Because the Friends of Algonquin Park have produced such an excellent series of inexpensive books dealing with Algonquin, a separate section is devoted to their books.

Publications of the Friends of Algonquin Park

I highly recommend all of the Friends' publications as excellent sources of information on specific aspects of Algonquin. Many are applicable to other regions as well. Visit the Friends' website, www.algonquinpark.on.ca, for all of their publications and products, as well as membership information.

The following is a partial list of many of the publications that I find particularly useful. I have not listed the Trail Guide booklets, which cover all of Algonquin's interpretive trails. The Friends' products are not only exceptionally well done but also are incredibly inexpensive. For example, *Birds of Algonquin Provincial Park* contains 89 colour photographs and at the time of writing sells for a mere $2.95.

Natural History
The Best of the Raven (Strickland, D. and R.J. Rutter, 1996)

Birds of Algonquin Provincial Park (Strickland, D., 2002)

Butterflies of Algonquin Provincial Park (Gard, W.O., 1994)

Checklist of the Bryophytes of Algonquin Provincial Park (Crins, W.J. and S. Darbyshire, 1993)

Checklist of the Conspicuous Fungi of Algonquin Provincial Park (Thorn, G., 2006)

Checklist of the Lichens of Algonquin Provincial Park (Dickson, H.L. and W.J. Crins, 1993)

Checklist and Seasonal Status of the Birds of Algonquin Provincial Park (Tozer, R., 2007)

Checklist and Seasonal Status of the Butterflies of Algonquin Provincial Park (Jones, C.D., 2003)

Checklist of the Vascular Plants of Algonquin Provincial Park (Crins, W.J., S. Blaney and D.F. Brunton, 1998)

A Field Guide to the Dragonflies and Damselflies of Algonquin Provincial Park and the Surrounding Area (Jones, C.D., M.L. Holder, A.L. Kingsley and P.S. Burke, 2008)

Fishes of Algonquin Provincial Park (Mandrak, N. and E.J. Crossman, 2003)

Fishing in Algonquin Provincial Park (Strickland, D., 2002)

Insects of Algonquin Provincial Park (Marshall, S., 1997)

Mammals of Algonquin Provincial Park (Strickland, D. and R.J. Rutter, 2002)

Mushrooms of Algonquin Provincial Park (Thorn, G., 2006)

The Raven Talks About Wolves (Strickland, D., 2002)

The Raven Talks About Deer and Moose (Strickland, D. 2003)

The Raven Talks About Fish and Lakes (Strickland, D. 2004)

Reptiles and Amphibians of Algonquin Provincial Park (Brooks, R., D. Strickland and R.J. Rutter, 2003)

Trees of Algonquin Provincial Park (Strickland, D., 2006)

Wildflowers of Algonquin Provincial Park (Strickland, D. and J. LeVay, 1998)

Wolf Howling in Algonquin Provincial Park (Strickland, D., 2004)

Human History

Algonquin Story (Saunders Miller, A., 2003)

Born at Brule Lake, Algonquin Park (McCormick Pigeon, M., 1995)

A Chronology of Algonquin Provincial Park (MacKay, R., 2002)

Early Days in Algonquin Park (Addison, O., 2006)

Glimpses of Algonquin (Garland, G.D., 1994)

Joe Lavalley and the Paleface (Wicksteed, B., 2003)

Living at Cache Lake (McCormick Pigeon, M,. 1995)

More About the Blacksmith Shop (MacKay, R., 1997)

Paddling my Own Canoe (Keyser, E.S., 2005)

Pictorial History of Algonquin Provincial Park (Tozer, R. and D. Strickland, 2004)

Whitney: St. Anthony's Mill Town on Booth's Railway (Westhouse B.D., 2003)

Canoeing in Algonquin

Canoe Routes of Algonquin Provincial Park (2007)
Madawaska River and Opeongo River Whitewater Guide (Drought, G., 2003)

Petawawa River Whitewater Guide (Drought, G., 2005)

The Canoeist's Manual (Stringer, O., 2004)

Miscellaneous Publications and Products

Acid Rain in Algonquin Provincial Park (Strickland, D., 1993)

Algonquin Provincial Park Bibliography (Tozer, R. and N. Checko, 2006)

Backpacking Trails of Algonquin Provincial Park (2007)

Lake Depth Maps of Algonquin Provincial Park (Betteridge, G. and B. Monroe, 2003)

Names of Algonquin Provincial Park (Garland, G.D., 1997)

Voices of Algonquin (CD) (Gibson, D.W. and R. Tozer, 2005)

Other Publications

Algonquin Park Pictorials

Runtz, M. *Algonquin Souvenir* (Erin: Boston Mills Press, 2007)

Camping and Canoeing

Callan, K. *A Paddler's Guide to Algonquin Park* (Erin: Boston Mills Press, 2004)

Callan, K. *The Happy Camper: An Essential Guide to Life Outdoors* (Erin: Boston Mills Press, 2005)

Lloyd, D.L. *Canoeing Algonquin Park* (Toronto: Hushion House, 2000)

Carpenter, D. *A Camper's Guide to Ontario's Best Parks* (Erin: Boston Mills Press, 2005)

Human History

Bice, R. *Along the Trail in Algonquin Park* (Toronto: Natural Heritage/Natural History Inc., 2001)

Clemson, G. *Algonquin Voices: Selected Stories of Canoe Lake Women* (Victoria: Trafford, 2002)

Clemson, G. *Rock Lake Station* (Victoria: Trafford, 2005)

Clemson, G. *Treasuring Algonquin* (Victoria: Trafford, 2006)

Connelly, B.A. *Holy Old Whistlin': Yarns about Algonquin Park Loggers* (Burnstown: General Store, 2006)

Gage, S.R. *A Few Rustic Huts: Ranger Cabins and Logging Camp Buildings of Algonquin Park* (Oakville: Mosaic Press, 1985)

Lloyd, D.L. *Algonquin Harvest: The History of the McRae Lumber Mill* (Whitney: R.D. McRae, 2006)

MacKay, I. *Over the Hills to Georgian Bay* (Erin: Boston Mills Press, 1981)

MacKay, R. *Spirits of the Little Bonnechere: A History of Exploration, Logging, and Settlement 1800–1920* (Pembroke: Friends of Bonnechere Parks, 2002)

Mackey, D. and P. Mackey. *The Fossmill Story* (Toronto: University of Toronto Press, 1999)

Shaw, B. *Lake Opeongo* (Burnstown: General Store, 1998)

Wright, E.H. *Trail Blazers of Algonquin Park* (Eganville: HEW Enterprises, 2003)

Wright, E.H. Joe Lake: *Reminiscences of an Algonquin Park Ranger's Daughter* (Eganville: HEW Enterprises, 2000)

Natural History Publications

Theberge, J.B. *Wolf Country* (Toronto: McClelland & Stewart, 1998)

Quinn, N. *Algonquin Wildlife: Lessons in Survival* (Toronto: Natural Heritage/Natural Heritage Inc., 2002)

Identification Guides for Flora and Fauna

These identification guides are my current favourites for identifying plants and animals not only in Algonquin Park but also further afield. Many more books are available and new ones and new editions appear periodically.

Amphibians and Reptiles

MacCulloch, R.D. *The ROM Field Guide to Amphibians and Reptiles of Ontario* (Toronto: ROM/McClelland & Stewart, 2002)

Birds

Dunn, J.L. and J. Alderfer. *Field Guide to the Birds of North America* (Washington: National Geographic Society, 2006)

Peterson, R.T. *Birds of Eastern and Central North America* (New York: Houghton Mifflin, 2002)

Sibley, D.A. *The Sibley Guide to Birds of Eastern North America* (New York: Alfred A. Knopf, 2003)

Ferns

Cobb, B., C. Lowe and E. Farnsworth. *Ferns of Northeastern and Central North America* (New York: Houghton Mifflin, 2005)

Geology

Ahern, Frank. A*lgonquin Park through Time and Space* (Toronto: Warwick, 2006)

Eyles, N. *Ontario Rocks* (Toronto: Fitzhenry & Whiteside, 2002)

Insects

Brock, J.P. and K. Kaufman. *Kaufman Field Guide to Butterflies of North America* (New York: Houghton Mifflin, 2003)

Covell, C.V. *A Field Guide to the Moths of Eastern North America* (Martinsville: Virginia Museum of Natural History, 2005)

Lamb, L. *Damselflies of the Northeast* (New York: Biodiversity Press, 2004)

Mead, K. *Dragonflies of the North Woods* (Duluth: Kollath-Stensaas, 2003)

Reid, G. et al. *Golden Guide to Pond Life* (New York: St. Martin's Press, 2001)

Wagner, D.L. *Caterpillars of Eastern North America* (Princeton: Princeton University Press, 2005)

Lichens

Brodo, E., S.D. Sharnoff and S. Sharnoff. *The Lichens of North America* (New Haven: Yale University Press, 2001)

Mammals

Eder, T. *Mammals of Ontario* (Winnipeg: Lone Pine, 2002)

Reid, F.A. *Mammals of North America* (New York: Houghton Mifflin, 2006)

Mushrooms

Barron, G. *Mushrooms of Ontario and Eastern Canada* (Winnipeg: Lone Pine, 1999)

Spiders

Weber, L. *Spiders of the North Woods* (Duluth: Kollath-Stensaas, 2003)

Trees and Shrubs

Kershaw, Linda. *Trees of Ontario* (Winnipeg: Lone Pine, 2001)

Soper, J.H. and M.L. Heimburger. *Shrubs of Ontario* (Toronto: Royal Ontario Museum, 1982)

Wildflowers

Newcomb, L. *Newcomb's Wildflower Guide* (Boston: Little, Brown, 1977)

Peterson, R.T. and M. McKenny. *A Field Guide to Wildflowers of Northeastern and North-Central North America* (New York: Houghton Mifflin, 1968)

INDEX

Beauty is a hallmark of Algonquin in all seasons, at all times of day.

An Algonquin sunset is never complete without the wild cries of loons.